Read

HERE THEY COME

Rebounding from Life's Pitfalls and   Ascending into a Life Worth Living.

It's not homework...

It's just pearls to live by for teenagers and young adults who want to live their best life!

By Dr. Bridget Isaac

Ready or Not, Here They Come

Atlanta, Georgia

Dedication

This book is dedicated to my mother, Ella Jo Owens-Goodman.
What can I say, she has been the most phenomenal mother and woman ever imagined. As much as I write, I will never be able to find the words to thank you for your love, patience, generosity, and tons of advice. I love you and so happy that God made you... *just for me.*

#THE BEST MOM ON THE PLANET

The Conversation Starters

Table Of Contents

Let the Games Begin

People have often compared the game of life with chess. The mastery and the winning all come with having forethought and calculation.

In life, most, if not all, have a fair chance at winning. Your harlequin board with all its majesty and regalia is equipped with the queen and king which exemplify expert communication and planning. In the use of these well-developed skills, your *moves* are never haphazard and without consideration.

You are prepared to fight and win this game of life with purpose. You know and understand your purpose. You can either ingeniously use it to influence some or detract others. Your purpose is the Bishop on your board as it keenly alerts others of the core of your existence.

You already know that you won't have a cheering squad who will always be there to cheer you on or encourage you to carry on, but you learn how to use your piece of self-esteem to aid you in mastering your purpose. That piece on your life's game-board called self-control is a critical piece to your success in life as it holds the capacity to not only end your life, but the lives of others. Your game starts at a tremendous deficit if you have no self-control.

Your final move to impose a checkmate or perhaps win a championship ring, jacket, trophy, or some other award… it all culminates around your relationships. These are the platinum pawns on your game-board. If you ever expect to win at the game of life, you must invest the time to cultivate your relationships so that they are always in place to help you win the game.

In life, you will at times need to show your practical skills, creative mastery, and intellectual capacity for so many different things. Now that you are aware of the challenges which are sure to prey upon spectrums of your life experiences, you can see the winner's circle.

Just remember this:

In all things, secure and guard the Queen. Deliberately communicating things that are positive, cautious, and sober in nature. Protect the direction of your Rook as it holds the dreams and hopes of your life's purpose. No matter the situation you may find yourself in, use a clear mind while positioning your Bishop and Knight. This illuminates a clear path to a triumphant win using self-control and self-esteem.

Successful navigation through life continues with your Pawn (s) by your side. Although many may not value the Pawn, you understand that the Pawn is extremely valuable as it represents your closest and most endearing relationships.

2

Then... our KING, whom you should never trade, shall be revered as priceless. Although every game hasn't even started, you now realize that you have all of the pieces to win the games of life as our KING is always right there on the board... on deck to HELP YOU WIN EVERY GAME.

So, let the games begin.

B. Isaac

Forward

Thank you for purchasing my first book.
You are appreciated!!

Woven throughout the following pages, my intention is to add an unyielding link to the chain that *binds* the millennials to the rest of us. In today's world, our young people are a force to be reckoned with. So many are smart, quick, innovative, and brave. As in any other generation, the millennials are power packed with energy, ideas, and the guts to take on just about anything. More than ever, this generation wants to call the shots. They want to take care of themselves and help their families while working a job, going to school, or collecting a few coins on social media.

It's true, social media platforms have provided viable business opportunities for our youth especially if they have ample followers. You're right, some are doing much more than taking and posting selfies. Today, young adults are not afraid to start their own businesses. Many have figured out that they can use their gifts and talents to actually become independent and truly self-sufficient. **FACTS**.... I am convinced that there has never been a time before now that people under the age of 25 have earned the substantial amounts of income as what's being reported by so many young people today. If they don't start a business, a good portion of millennials are truly anxious to work.

This book describes the likeness of various young people who I have crossed paths with throughout my career. As an educator and certified life coach, I have worked in high schools, middle schools, and juvenile correctional facilities. This translates to having worked with primarily urban youth who are from disadvantaged and disenfranchised communities. To make it plain, my students have largely hailed from lower socio-economic backgrounds and therefore have been consumed with *survival rather than studying*.

Ready or Not Here They Come takes a snapshot of the frustrations, fears, hopes, and anxieties expressed by millennials preparing to graduate from high school. As a direct result of the random conversations, spontaneous comments, collective feedback and debates, I felt compelled to write this manuscript to hopefully *keep the key conversations and critical thinking going*. So here you have it, a paperback compiled with memories of some of the most *imperative* Bonafide Talk sessions I've ever had with teenagers in my entire career.

It didn't take long to figure out that the millennials had significant questions and interest in such topics as self-esteem, peer pressure, anger management, and relationships. Usually, it didn't take much for the millennials to get off task and attempt to stay there. So, the stories here actually pick up where the brief conversations, crazy comments, laughs, and serious debates left off. In

view of the youngsters who often think and act with unapologetic emotion and quick responsiveness, I offered the quintessential parking lot. If you're wondering how in the world a parking lot can help anyone grow, heal, and change… most students know that a classroom parking lot is where they can post or park their sticky notes with questions, thoughts, or criticism about any and everything worthy of examination or defense. The thoughts and ideas shared here are offered to help adolescents, teenagers, and young adults win in life. It's a **Self Help Book** that can help you pave your own yellow brick road to the life you've envisioned for yourself. The pearls found in this book are a treasure chest for those who are searching for their best life. Basically, I hope that you enjoy the occasional chats, thought provoking discussions, information, and caution shared in this body of work. If you are between the ages of 13 and 25… in the words of a famous television talk show host who hails from *Jersey*…

"You are my people!"

Across a twenty-year span of working with youth of all ages, I have had the best time working with teenagers and young adults. They just never seem to shy away from some of the most candid, riveting, and utterly transparent conversations ever. Some called it… "keeping it real or keeping it 100". I call it keeping it **Bonafide**. In the end, this book has been written not only for the millennial, pre-teen, or young adult, but also parents and professionals who

can use some of the conversations described in this text as *conversation starters* with someone of this generation or younger.

In this scroll, millennials and others will find a ton of anecdotes and knowledge that can help them navigate a path to living their best life. Hopefully, this playbook will be one of the millennial's big secrets for living a victorious life.

Happy Reading,

Bridget Isaac, Ed.D., MSW

Chapter 1:
Who is Dr. Isaac?

Trying to describe myself is tough. The one thing I can say with great confidence is that I just took a DNA test and found out that I am the woman with a treasure chest of great ideas for something. You name it, I have it. I'm creative that way. I have loads of passion for people and enjoy helping to developing things that will be found as useful or perhaps beneficial. I love the idea of being a reliable resource for others. If it involves developing programs, workshops, seminars, media productions or anything which merges education, the arts, and entertainment together that will ultimately have a positive impact on people... I am ALL-IN.

I have deep and unwavering concerns about the wellness of people, in particular today's youth...**360 degree wellness**. This may justify why I have such genuine concern for my students and wanting to stay abreast of things happening in their young world. I would frequently check-in with my students, asking them about nothing more than themselves and their assessment of how life was treating them. I enjoy understanding and learning the culture of our younger generations. Having a personality that is far from shy, introverted, or reticent makes it very easy for me to engage anyone who has a pulse. Yes, I enjoy meeting people and will invite everyone to my personal party. All it takes is to

respect everyone, maintain integrity in everything you do, have patience, and a great sense of humor. I love to laugh. So, I am that lady who laughs out loud as often as possible.

Now… my *think tank* best friend/sister calls me gregarious and loquacious. Whaaaaaat????????

Okay, so I like to talk. Some say I talk a lot. Whatever. At least I have plenty to say that makes good sense.

Anyway, she says that I'm fearless, head strong, determined, personable, polite, and down to earth. Anita calls me passionate about responding to the realities and needs of at-risk youth. In her words, she said "I never give up on kids." One coworker calls me a serious advocate for children. What can I say, I have faith in my kids and tend to be extremely empathetic about their situations and personal journeys. Honestly, I'm that lady who is deeply concerned about things that will help to change the trajectory of our urban youth. I believe our kids will go far when given the right opportunities and exposed to innovative and meaningful experiences in and outside of the classroom. I am driven to find the most *uncommon* ways to positively impact students who may not have a mentor, family member, or anyone else that can help make their journey a little more enjoyable, if not productive and efficient.

Chapter 2:
No Worries, I GOT YOU!

For anyone who thinks having a life coach is a pretty good idea… wonderful. Since were not meeting face to face this book hopes to *inspire you* rather than give advice. The information shared is given to help you make *better decisions* and *better choices* for living your best life… an incredible life.

Here recently, my high school students have started calling me the Millennial Life Coach (MLC). I've worked with teenagers for more than half of my teaching career. In that time, I've taught Language Arts and listened to teenagers discussing and/or writing their thoughts, feelings, concerns, complaints, worries, frustrations, and ideas about countless topics. What can I say? I was always available to listen and then give heart felt advice whenever asked… no matter the topic.

In time, it became evident that students actually enjoyed having serious conversations with me. Since I wasn't being paid to lead group sessions or act as their life coach, counselor or school social worker, I honestly listened a whole lot and in turn urged students to "think" about what was being stated by their peers and to consider sound, mature, and positive resolutions to the dilemmas they heard. This is how I became privy to what kids were

thinking, how they felt, and what was truly important to them. If I could share a golden nugget with anyone who desires to establish a meaningful and worthwhile relationship with a millennial… you must respect what they have to say, be transparent about your own feelings and thoughts, and never judge them for the mistakes made. I know I made that sound easy, but it really is that easy. As I spent so much time talking with my students and truly having the most incredible conversations with them, it wasn't long before I was saying… "Guys, we can't keep spending all this time talking about stuff. I can't help but tell you some really important stuff. How about I put it all in a book? How does that sound???"

Why did I say that? As I began writing, they encouraged me to keep going, keep adding things and more topics. It was crazy. Some would remind me of things to add that I had not previously included. So, I am proud to say that my students firmly understood that this book was being written with the sole purpose of helping teenagers and other young people who were dealing with the same or similar things as they were. Hopefully, many youngsters will benefit from the information shared in this ultimate playbook for today's millennials.

This playbook is being published at the beginning of a brand-new decade. It's 2020. Incidentally, we are currently sitting in a season of TALK. Everybody wants to talk now. Lucky for me, I've always been a talker who finds it easy

to engage practically anyone in a conversation. It's true... I know NO strangers. In realizing that so many of our kids just didn't care to talk or really communicate their feelings and thoughts with others, I became very interested in wanting to hear their feelings and thoughts about things that were important to them. I wanted them to talk more, debate, and critically think about things in their world today. I wanted them to learn and understand how to resolve their own issues by having authentic communication with others.

Over the years, many of my young stars and scholars have demonstrated strong toastmaster qualities as future public speakers and debaters. It's amazing how hard I have laughed at the things they would say. Some kids just don't know when they have a natural gift for comedy. It was intriguing to see my teenagers offer comments that were thoughtful and sincere. And I can genuinely say that my students hardly ever crossed the line of being disrespectful, unsympathetic, or non-empathetic. If someone made that mistake, they'd know to not let that happen again.

The kids were typically so comfortable in my classroom that it took nothing for them to pose personal questions or share comments about everything under the sun. Conversations became so interesting that to protect student confidentiality, I encouraged students to just give me their topic of interest on a post-it note and we could revisit the topic at another time. Since we never really had the time or

space to properly or ethically unwrap the appropriate coping and behavioral health skills necessary for success in high school and beyond, I decided to write this book to make good on my promise to share information that responds to their questions, concerns, and interest. Generally, teens would write out their question or concerns on plain white paper. Whatever their interest were, it had to be shared anonymously. No doubt, someone would just stand and blurt out his or her frustrations not caring about the concept of remaining anonymous. Truth be told, many students had no problem with speaking openly. There was no judgement, so students felt safe speaking their minds.

Dear Dr. MLC (*millennial life coach*) instantly became a popular way for shy, curious, introverted, puzzled, and perplexed teens to fire away with a host of anonymously written questions and scenarios for me to dissect and evaluate. During small group chats, topics were randomly selected for group discussions and analysis. Again and again, absent students were so anxious to learn what our discussions covered during their absence, that they needed updates upon their return to class. Students hated missing out on our proverbial fire side chats. One little question and they'd take off with comments, elevated voices, some laughter, and smiles. Those smiling were reacting to the energy and excitement of the students who were determined to be heard. Some students would walk around the room as they shared out. Completely unashamed and very aware of their audience.

Just babies being Amazing!

The dynamics of the group always made it interesting to see how conversations would unfold. The teens were so wide open. They had no care, no concern, no fear, and no bridle. Some kids would tell me, "You know they call millennials savages." "No... I didn't know that. Why do you think that is?????" Then we're off into another discussion that ultimately resembled a condensed conversation about learning how to ignore people and not to answer or respond to whatever people call you. Going one or two steps further, I'd drop a few pearls while inquiring how does behavior, attitude, self- control or lack of it, your communication, self-respect, or respect for others might imply a few things that may or may not be true about a person. No doubt. One or two beautiful souls would boldly admit, "Naaaw its right. We can be savages."

In my head I'm thinking, "For Real? No, he didn't just say that."

Constant and non-stop comments were made which typically forced me to get students to think deeply about the things they were saying. Students reaching out to *Dr. MLC* on their little yellow post-it notes were primarily seeking advice about their relationships with a girl friend or boyfriend; feelings of depression; frequent feelings of anger and frustration; fear of rampant violence in their community; feelings of apprehension in starting new

relationships; how to improve one's ability to trust others; and the challenges of having low self-esteem and poor body image.

The many, many statements and discussions fueled by their comments have inspired me to write this book. My millennials are awesome. Most of them are very witty and always on cue to make thought-provoking statements that require my "nonjudgmental adult" attention and serious intervention. Everyone has an opinion and if you are fortunate enough to hear the unfiltered thoughts and feelings of today's teenager or young adult be prepared to lose your lace front wig or toupee just hearing them talk about their life, problems, concerns, and needs.

At the end of the day,

this book hopes to start or at least continue important conversations that are relevant to the growth and maturity of our youth.

All youth deserve to know how to address or resolve every difficult predicament they might find themselves in. Ideally, every youth should take time to connect with a trusted adult and mentor whom you can talk to. Once you've found a mature, respected, professional, and highly transparent person to talk with… allow them to stand as a buffer between you and the difficult things you may be facing. *Ready or Not, Here They Come* gives young people the opportunity to reflect on key elements that promote

their BEST health, wellness, personal stability, and balance in their adult life. Simply put, this book gets the ball rolling towards gaining the help and motivation anyone might need to move them into the winner's circle. So without further ado enjoy this BonaFide Talk that will hopefully prove to be timeless as generations begin to chop it up, evaluate, or chew over these topics at home, school, and everywhere else they go.

Talk talk talk talk talk talk talk talk talk that's my heart's desire for today's millennial. After all, that's the only way anyone will ever be clear about what you're thinking or what's important to you. What you think- does matter. You matter. Over the next several chapters, you will see exactly what many teenagers and young adults are talking about or really want to talk about more with an adult who is respected, nonjudgmental, and caring. Wherever you fit in that equation, pull up a chair, read, and talk-about-it.

Chapter 3:
Introduction

As it relates to the game of chess, we have used it as a metaphor to gleam a deeper understanding of how we should all navigate through life. Chess is a game of strategy where you think of moves well in advance far ahead of your opponent. You are ten steps ahead of the average bear. When you take time to compare the chess game with life, it certainly makes perfect sense. In life, when you want to win or experience a reasonable level of success you must think ahead. You must plan "your show". Simply put, you should and must plan *what-you-show*. Your work, attire, language, and personality all can apply.

That's good stuff!!

Seriously, you must plan things out in your life. Don't fly by the seat of your pants just waiting for things to fall out of the sky and subsequently into your lap. Think ahead, anticipate the things you will need to do and be good at. Once you've taken time to pay attention to other people who are on the ball, you should begin to understand what others might do to be on top of their game. This kind of forethought can certainly give you a good advantage when having to survive highly competitive or stressful situations.

In comparison to life, each game piece represents *six critical skills* that everyone should master in order to join the winners circle in life. The tenets of this book bring a laser focus to **communication, planning, purpose, self-esteem, self-control, and relationships.** These skills are seen as the six most important elements of having a balanced and fulfilling life. Nothing is a guarantee, however it is presumed that your odds at winning in life are increased substantially when you possess these qualities. Of course there are other important skills that I would encourage any young person to familiarize themselves with, such as having patience, tolerance, and good judgment. No need to worry because you will certainly improve these skills as you grow older and gain a few miles on your journey. Just know that the characteristics mentioned and explored here applied best when considering the conversations, comments, and questions posed by the millennials I know.

It should not be a stretch to think that having good communication skills is the number one trait to have in one's arsenal of personal competencies. Yes, it is important to know how to talk, when to talk, and what to say. Seriously, in order to connect with and understand others, we must begin this process by having a laser focus on how to appropriately articulate, express, and assert what we are thinking, feeling, and doing. It's all about talking. Talk, talk, talk, talk, talk. I believe smart people can absolutely think and talk at the same time the same as being able to

walk and chew gum. No one should have to guess what's on your mind. There's something that needs to be said about anyone who feels *a certain-kinda-way* about something or someone but feels there is no reasonable platform to express your feelings.''

Its true, countless scholars agree that many young and older millennials spend considerable if not inexcusable amounts of time texting and not talking. So, the cat is out of the bag. Millennials spend extensive and huge amounts of time on their phones, tablets, laptops, and computers. It's been reported for years that using technology to such an extreme degree actually thwarts and impedes the basic skill of conversing or perhaps disagreeing with someone.

For obvious reasons, the research that exist on the importance of communication skills merely implies that it is a key attribute to advancing change, positive results, answers, and resolutions in our life. When you sit and think about our world today, would you agree that circumstances could have been a lot more favorable had someone talked it out- before they walked or acted out what they were thinking? Talking and communicating most definitely helps us to avoid having a rush to judgment, snap or sometimes deadly response to things that irritate us.

Planning and setting goals for yourself is a critical attribute to have as well. You must be unforgiving about what it is that you'd like to accomplish in life. Take time to truly discover what will work best for you in your life at this

time. This moment in time. Make up your mind that this time, you will do exactly what you set out to do. *No excuses and no delays.* Be in a hurry to experience your best self. You're a piece of art. A masterpiece created by *God.* So, how do you want to showcase this phenomenal, extraordinary you? Planning the big reveal is the beginning of your journey to realizing your Best Life.

What do you want the world to see? What do you want the world to know about you? What are the one or two things that make you special or make you stand out? Before you think to answer with the word "nothing," consider the fact that you were created by *God* and to say "nothing" is a complete and utter insult to the Almighty. In the case you didn't know it, or never heard it... *God* is only in the business of making masterpieces. It's your free will that creates or sustains the platform you allow your masterpiece to shine, thrive, or tarnish.

There are so many reasons and explanations that a person gives to discount or denounce their royal craftsmanship and this is a huge mistake. No matter what challenges we may have to face in life, it's incumbent of us to "Find A Way or Make A Way". Specifically, we must find ways to survive, exist, and dwell amongst others <u>without</u> discoloring, rusting, or perhaps disgracing our royal being. We are all magnificent and noble in some way. Every living and breathing individual has something incredible to offer the world. If you don't know what that is yet, no worries.

While reading this book, you will find out what that incredibly special thing is.

If you have never done so before, I highly recommend that you start your planning process with using a vision board to pin point every idea, dream, or desire you have for your life. Outline or layout what you would like to experience or realize in your life over a span of time. You might start by making deliberate plans for the **next** year, two, three, five, ten, or twenty years of your life. Your dreams are important here. Consider how long it may take to accomplish your dream.

Now that you've thought of a timeline, write down your personal responsibilities, the resources, and people needed to capture or live your dream. It's okay to have one or more dreams. We all have them. Consider this, a person who desires to lose weight, it's their dream to lose 50 pounds. However, they never plan out a diet, start an exercise routine, or become mentally prepared to accomplish the goal. Same difference for you. Anything you want to accomplish in your life must be *strategically* planned out and held as a personal truth until it is accomplished. ...Just like playing the game of chess.

Finding and knowing your purpose will certainly inform others of the *plans* you are making, your ambitions, and important life pursuits. Some people have multiple plans in life (i.e. educational goals, career aspirations, family, health, finances, and social life which one day might include international travel). When considering all of these

things, an individual should come to some realization of what they *believe* they are born to do, accomplish, contribute to. If the idea of knowing or finding your purpose presents a quandary or dilemma, start with what you do best. What are you good at? What can you do very well with just about little or no assistance? Unpack that. Peel that onion until you figure out what you are already the bomb or dynamic at. What comes natural to you? That thing that comes natural to you should be something you can make a good honest living at. When you sit and really think about it with a sound, clear and mature mind, you realize that you could actually do quite well for yourself as an independent adult.

Answer these questions... Why are you here? What motivates you? What makes you feel most connected to other people? What things cause you to adjust your behavior, habits, and thoughts as it relates to a personal skill or talent you have?

Take a moment to think about these things. It's true, you will find your "purpose" sometimes hidden like a pearl in an oyster if you investigate long enough. Investigate. Take time to discover, ask questions, be curious, desire to learn everything about what you already have a natural gift for. The amazing thing is that every human being is his or her own pearl. You are an unique and precious gem. A jewel to be treasured. Everyone is a precious pearl to be admired, adorned, appreciated, and applauded for something. If you don't have any ideas about what your purpose might be,

take time to get into a quiet place and mind-space, meditate, pray and ask God to help you to discern what your purpose might be. You will gain insight into what it is about you that the world can benefit from. Be realistic and practical as you *introspectively* consider what path you should direct your adult journey in life. Look in-ward and find which interest, hobby, or occupation brings you the most peace and personal satisfaction.

Today, we use that word "truth" to express our core values. What do you value in life? In what ways does your life exemplify integrity, respect, and commitment? This is your truth? This thing called purpose virtually urges us to get real with ourselves and discover how you can be used in the world. What good service can you render? No, I'm not trying to preach, but hope to commission you to find out how you can help anyone else on earth besides you.

So, now that you have figured out your purpose, developing a plan for your life should be a lot easier. Writing your thoughts about how you can improve your interpersonal or communication skills will only help to create harmony in your life. Understanding how to engage others in appropriate and positive conversations simply invites peace, kinship, and understanding with others. This is a good thing. When we are trying to improve our communication skills, it's perfectly okay to practice our tone of voice, words, and facial expressions when communicating with others. You already know that use of profanity incites alarm and disrespect. Provoking or

agitating people in this way is sure to create an uncomfortable scenario for everyone involved. If you need to, work on this. Finding clear ways to express yourself without profanity shows that you can speak coherently with other intelligent people whom you may encounter on a job, in school, or other relationship. Respect in your speech is always a winner. Learn to talk-it-out before you walk-it-out. Actually, think-it-out before you talk-it-out. It's true, real Bosses, Queens, and Kings do that.

No Cap!!

Other important attributes our young millennials can consider sharpening are **self-esteem** and **self-control**. Later on, you will discover ways to gain more confidence and faith in yourself. Understanding how to restrain yourself or maintain self-control are other important attributes that will keep you on track for success and balance in your life. All of the personal traits mentioned here are seen as the chess pieces or skills needed to master the game of life. Mastery in the key skills mentioned are what everyone should be consistently aiming at in order to have a stress and drama free life. Ultimately, know that I am suggesting that effective life skills and meaningful relationships will fundamentally raise or increase the likelihood of you achieving a happy life.

YES...

YOUR HAPPINESS DOES MATTER!

Chapter 4:
First Things First

 # How to Improve My Communication Skills

Making a conscious effort to communicate more effectively in your daily speech and writing will most certainly improve your capacity to exchange ideas, your thoughts, and solve problems. Being a good or pretty decent communicator absolutely requires that you take a moment to think about what you want to say before you speak. **No Cap.** Be quiet first. Then speak second.

You'd be surprised how many misunderstandings, fights and arguments that would never happen if people thought about what was coming out of their mouth first. Real Talk. Think about it. So, if your serious about being at your best when it comes to expressing yourself at school, work, and home try doing a lot more listening, thinking, then speaking. If things could potentially go in a direction you would rather they not, then always consider possible consequences to everything… including your speech and actions. When I am truly angry about something, it is likely that I will not just blast-off. I believe everyone, including myself must keep a cool head at all times. Just relax. Never let your emotions completely sabotage or take over a situation.

Improved communication skills are indicative of speech and writing that tends to include more detailed information, thoughts, feelings, facts, and ideas. Getting a grasp on expressing yourself in the most positive way is definitely a winner. It's perfectly okay to talk more, express positivity, and engage others with conversations that relate to school activities, entertainment, community events, and local news. Yes, learn to talk more to connect with others around you at school, home, and your community. Start training yourself to express positivity even if you're not feeling positive or cheerful. You're right, you probably won't wake up every morning with a smile on your face and a song in your heart, however, everyone around you doesn't have to know it.

Real talk… sometimes it takes certain people a little while longer to wake up in the morning and get into the groove of their normal day. In case you don't know it, there are many adults who refuse to officially start their day without a cup of coffee. So whether it's coffee, some other beverage, a favorite food, exercise, or radio station that can get you ready for your day, it's a good idea to use it. Establish a *positive routine* to help you get and stay in a positive and productive frame of mind all day.

Pin pointing a positive daily routine will rely completely on your awareness and usage of a wide variety of activities, such as hours of sleep each night, reading before bed, meditation, prayer, exercise, journal writing, listening to

music or podcast, and planning a daily schedule with the assignments, exams, work duties, and other activities you have. Good habits which foster or inspire you to be productive can only help you stay on track for other things you are striving to accomplish in your life. Once you begin to utilize at least five of your top positive habits to start each day, it will become easier for you to gain clarity about your dreams and hopes for the future.

 # Planning and Setting Goals

By now, you may be able to tell that I am a strong advocate for writing things down and making plans for just about everything. When you take time to plan things, you're more likely to be organized. If you're organized, you're less likely to miss the things that are important. So get into the habit of writing things down with a time frame in which you'd like to complete certain task. Practice these strategies and "believe" that the results will work in your favor. Being proactive in planning just about everything is simply another way to set small goals or smart goals for yourself.

Start planning your daily schedules, then setting goals for the month, year and eventually your life. Remember that setting goals is a great habit to have. It is also important to monitor your progress as you strive to achieve your goals. Logically, if it's hard for you to successfully meet a goal that you've set for the day, week, or month, try changing your goals. When you are planning your goals ensure that they are realistic according to your available resources,

time, or finances. As you make smaller goals, then it's smart to plan on achieving larger goals. Life planning can ultimately include post-secondary education, career, family, financial, or perhaps health. The strategies you use to "plan" your life are the things that will help you to successfully realize your dreams, aspirations, and visions for your future.

Chapter 5:
Finding Your Purpose

Getting busy with planning and setting small goals for yourself can open a window for you to realize your purpose in life. Think about it, when you sit and map out all the things you enjoy doing and are passionate about doing, these things give you insight into your life's purpose. Along with planning for our success in life, we must figure out what our purpose or existence in life looks like. If you haven't figured out your purpose yet, don't feel bad because there are a lot of people of every age on the planet who have not figured out "their purpose" in life.

Putting a zoom lens on this thing called purpose requires that you take some notes about all the things that inspire you, give you energy, bring you joy, a sense of fulfillment, and uniqueness. Finding your purpose will involve you doing some unpacking. No, you're not unpacking a learning standard per se, but taking time to discover how your natural skills and innate ability can be used for others to enjoy or benefit. So now is the time for you to take time investigating, asking yourself questions and providing honest answers to those questions.

What is it about your gift or purpose that makes you stand out from anyone else you know personally? How can your purpose be used to help edify, uplift, or strengthen someone

else? Can the world use your talent, skill, or gift today? If there were any great skill set, know-how, job, expertise, or proficiency you wish you had... what would it be?

What is a job you believe you could do with your eyes practically closed with mastery or some high level of proficiency? Basically... you realize that you have some "real skills" in this.

These are the things that speak to your purpose. What skills are you really good at? Which skills would you like to further develop and make better than what they are right now? Whatever it is that you do well with passion, time, dedication, heart, and serious thought... this is a strong indication of your purpose.

As you reflect on these things that you do well, remember that the potter aka Almighty God has used superior craftsmanship to build, mold, shape, and decorate you. That's why we're all different down to our finger tips and their prints. Never forget that God is a master potter who is unmatched and never duplicated. Keep in mind that you were created with maximum durability to be appreciated by many. Absorb that thought and consider all of the people you know and how many truly appreciate you for being you... your friendship, skills, or gift you share with the world.

Trying to get a handle on your purpose and true calling will require patience and time to devote to understanding your

capacity for responding to a need of people in your community, a business, or school. You've got to be calm, dedicated to mastering your skills, and persistent as you believe that your prayers for discernment will be answered. Oftentimes, getting what you prayed for or what you need won't happen instantly. So you can't be in a big ridiculous hurry to get some of the things you've prayed for or perhaps put in your journal. Continue to believe and know that God has a way to make sure that you get access to everything you need... just *believe* that he can and he will do it.

This game we sometimes call life has bold and heavy pieces to be moved around its chess board. We are constantly moving, shifting, pulling, tussling, jerking, or pushing our way through life with our eyes on the prize of winning. Your game board is adorned with many colors, textures, and sizes offering you a field of accomplishments, disappointments, victories, and failures alike. This game consistently challenges you every step of the way to *answer the call* for duty and purpose.

If you want to become a part of the winner's circle with championship rings, belts, medals, ribbons, jackets, or trophies... find your purpose. In my opinion, one thing is certain... your calling, duty, or charge is to help or serve mankind. Plain and simple. Whatever you do well or perhaps exceptional is often referred to as your *calling or purpose*. Taking this into consideration, you should know

that your purpose has everything to do with helping your royal tapestry to shine. Remember you were created to help advance the good work of GOD Almighty who made you. Yes, I said good work. **Hint...** you should be thinking of a "Good" work you can do with your purpose.

Unfortunately, there are many who never seem to find their good or positive potential due to the sheer pain, hurt, or anguish they may be feeling in life. There are some people who become so consumed with negative feelings, self-defeating behavior, anger, and self-doubt that they never find their royalty. Instead, they press on through life rationing out the same level of hurt that has been dumped onto them. It's true, hurt people... really do hurt people. It becomes a vicious cycle if you refuse to find the strength to talk with someone you trust about it. If you or someone you know is feeling overwhelming hurt and pain, please seek out help. There is HELP for everyone. Please see the resource guide in the back of this book for help with feeling, thinking, and doing better.

The time has come for you to know in your NOAH *(meaning you know that you know that you know without question or doubt)* what on earth you came here for or what you were born to accomplish while inhabiting the earth. If you really want to understand what your true calling or purpose in life is, start by looking at what you do exceptionally well. What are the things that at least five or more people appreciate or feel grateful that you are around

to do? There is always something about each of us that people find pleasant, likeable, endearing, or helpful.

OK, to make it somewhat easier think back on your days in school and how well you did in your favorite classes. Some of us preferred certain classes over others because of the level of anxiety and stress it caused at the mere thought or mention of a certain subject. You didn't want to read the textbook chapters and had no interest in the study group that someone pulled together. You wanted O-U-T out. Out of the class and out of having to make any firm commitment to learning information about the subject against your will. I Got it.

Now, what about the classes you couldn't wait to get to? You could add to group discussions and personal conversations with ease. You had fun and really didn't have a huge problem with all the extra homework. Whatever. No big deal. You knew you'd knock it out in no time. Be aware of your *purpose indicator light* shining in front of you. This light may be a subtle flash, but it is a hint all the same. Don't ignore it.

Invest more and more time into understanding what interest you most about the lessons, activities or projects you get. Explore it, cultivate, perfect it and see where it might lead. Investigate and find out which careers can use the skills you learned with ease and enjoyment. Yes, match your good grades with careers that will pay you for the skills you've learned in those classes. If you're not sure about the

careers that use certain skills, please talk with your teacher. Ask your guidance counselor and teachers about careers associated with various curriculum you are learning. You'll be so happy that you decided to ask questions about careers and the typical salary for whatever you're interested in.

The process of getting really good at something or becoming knowledgeable about a subject doesn't come over night. However, you can handle this grooming, growing, and purifying process with just a little bit of time and patience. Remember, you are a masterpiece. So it's gonna take a little time to make you show-room-ready. Perhaps you will someday be featured on billboards from sea to shining sea. Maybe we will see your name or work in lights prominently featured somewhere on 42nd street in Manhattan. Who knows? Just know that there's a big world waiting on you to share your best self and work that will always lead you straight to your Best Life. See the connection?

If you're looking for your best life, it's highly unlikely to happen in a microwave or quick, fast and in a hurry. Nope. So take out your crock-pot because you may need to let your purpose cook slowly. Just remember that to learn, understand, and activate all of the good seasonings needed to make your plate a gourmet experience will take a little time. Think... what is it about you that makes you a delicacy? Not a deli, but a delicacy! What makes you of fine quality? A good choice, superior in every respect of

the word. If you're not already on that level, search for something that will allow you to reach the fine quality level.

Remember to start with the things you can do well... having reasonable success with little to no real effort. It's true, these very things can point you in the direction of discovering a small piece of your life's purpose. Yes, the discoveries you make while reading this book are just the beginning of your path to unveiling something fulfilling, gratifying, and worthwhile in your life. Yep, your Best Life is on the horizon. Once you explore the possibilities of your purpose, you'll be one step closer to Living Your Best Life.

Now, there are some of you who don't believe you were called to do anything worthwhile or positive. We know that you are in the building... you will not be ignored. Ponder this, if you experience deep pride and positive joy in everything you do while walking freely with your head held high and not afraid or slightly worried that you may have committed a serious crime after doing whatever you do to contribute to our world... then I say, ROCK ON!! Now, if you're committing serious crimes in the face of believing you do it for survival. Nope. You get no pass with this one. Of course, you already knew that.

What I will share is that I wish I had the time to introduce you to all of the hundreds, thousands, if not more people who were in very similar circumstances as you and found a honest hustle. They hustled hard to come up. They did

small to large jobs to make a little something to make ends meet. They didn't hurt anyone or hate-on-anyone because their grind and game was locked on super max. People like that... I totally admire because they never gave up and did the *doggone* thing without disrupting or invading anyone else's life.

Pause right here.

I need you to *think* about your honest answer to the question of whether you are an invader, one who attacks, intrudes, or provokes others or are you a peaceful person? Do you have PEACE in your life... in your heart? These are important things to consider because there are so many of us who have no peace, young and old. I am convinced that if we want more peace in our world, we better sure nuff be about the business of finding out who needs peace and how *we* can help them find it. What can you do to bring a smile to someone else's face?

Again, no judgement and no indictment. Just TALK BONAFIDE... Some of you have already been through hell. You've weathered the storm. I just pray that it's over now and that the rough patch in your life is finally smooth. If it's not over and it gets harder and harder to figure it all out... to make the best decisions, please extend your hand to someone who will listen, hear, and help you. *Stop thinking that people can't help you.* Give people a chance because you may be pleasantly surprised. Some people are called to help or be helpers. Let's see, I would include medical

professionals, counselors, teachers, ministers, coaches, and most other public service providers. There really are people who are hard-wired to HELP somebody. So please find those people and give them a chance to shine. DEEP. There really is good help out here, just like there's good and great coaches.

I once found an **anonymous** quote that said:

> *"The Purpose of human life is to serve, and to show compassion and the will to help others."*

Whoop whoop...

In my opinion, whomever said that was *right on time*. I really don't think it would be a stretch to presume that probably a million people have said that at some point. I said that very thing to some degree quite a few times myself because it's the truth. At the end of the day, you've got to look at your strengths. ...What you do well. Once you've considered what it is that you do well, then determine how those skills can be used to help someone else. It's just that simple.

Consider this question, how are you going to help **TEAM GOD**?

Your creator needs your help here on earth. He really does. Lil' ole you. He needs you to be a shining light of support, comfort, and a source of security to someone or perhaps

many that need it. Look at your skill set and determine how many people you can provide a good work for. As you think about the direction you see your life going in, write your plan down. To understand how you will reach your end goal, writing things down is a *smart habit* to start with so that you know the reasons why different things are necessary for you to complete and do at this time.

Now, remember what I said earlier that there are some people who get thrown off track and start on a self-destructive path that does more harm than good to themselves and everyone they know. If you struggle with frequently making unpropitious, detrimental, or negative decisions... please find someone to talk to. Get someone you trust who can help you *think* things out.

In my lifetime, I have witnessed very unfortunate circumstances, including loss of life for students who stayed on the edge. No limits, no boundaries, no margins, and no bridle. People with no bridle, to make it BONA FIDE are seen as simply people who haven't learned how to keep themselves in check. They haven't quite figured out how to restrain themselves. Unfortunately, many unbridled people eventually find themselves bridled by the justice system or another unbridled individual. Imagine that.

Just please remember this, everyone has the capacity to control themselves and do both <u>right</u> and <u>wrong</u>. Usually, people know when they are doing wrong. Whether people try hard to be sneaky or come full throttle and do

something in the wide open... *they know*. So it's here when the universe determines what shall be your consequence. Let your mind consider what are some of the great consequences we face when we have intentionally done wrong or hurt others. I believe in my heart that we somehow never get away with hurting or dishonoring God's Property. *Again, my disclaimer is that we all belong to GOD.* When we mishandle what GOD has made, I know for sure there is a very tall lesson to be learned from that.

Ultimately...

Please consider that I am merely suggesting that we all work hard to stay on the right side of this living thing so that we can all experience our BEST LIFE. I bet many of you are thinking... I could do so much better if my husband, wife, boyfriend, or girlfriend didn't do blah, blah, blah. To me, that sounds like we're blaming other people for the lousy, crummy, unacceptable, or poor decisions *we've* made.

Let's pause for minute.

Remember... you have a purpose. Part of your job is to protect your purpose and allow your purpose to shine. If you happen to be in a relationship that chips away at your purpose... it's time to regroup and say deuces.

Chapter 6:
How the four P's spell READY.

As a life coach who has experienced a fair share of life's highways, roadways, and skyways, I must tell you that there are four words you need to think about and use every day. If you want to stay ready for any and everything life will throw your way, you've got to familiarize yourself with the **four P's**.

PRIORITIZE

PERSPECTIVE

PURPOSE

PRAYER

I like these **four P's** because I am convinced that without these very important elements in your personal make up, you will probably never realize or capture your best life. On this journey, you will find that from time to time multiple things will come up that could potentially disrupt your life. You've made a list, which includes loads of triggers for your stress or anxiety, they may include school, work, co-workers, parents, girlfriends, boyfriends, wives, husbands, or other family members. It can seem like your list of things to do never gets shorter or goes away. It just gets longer... and longer... and longer no matter what you

get done or scratch off the list. Here, you've got to *prioritize* the things on your list. So figure out what's most important and then plan to do whatever is first, second, third, and so on.

Keeping things in *perspective* can be a life saver. Remember, *perspective* is merely what or how different people feel or think about something. Always keep in mind that it's okay for two people to think differently about something. Going to blows because someone says the New York Giants are the best NFL team on the planet is coo-coo when someone else challenges your ideas by saying no, the Pittsburg Steelers, or The New Orleans Saints are the best ball club in the history of the sport. Let someone else tell it, a few will swear that the Atlanta Falcons are the best thing smokin'. Riiiiiiiiiiiiight. That's an interesting thought. I'm smiling because I live in Atlanta. But people, I'm from the New York Metropolitan area. I'm always gonna push up my home team... The Giants. No matter where I live. *Come on now. It's all good.*

Bottom line, everyone can have an opinion about everything on the planet.

WE are not the Boss of people's thoughts.

It's really okay to be passionate about our favorite sports teams and athletes. We just have to manage all the emotions we have vested in these seasonal performances. The point being made here is that respectfully and lovingly

you can disagree with anyone. People are entitled to have their own opinions about things. After-all, who... again left us the boss of people's thoughts?

No one will leave you the Boss of their thoughts. Absolutely no one. So if you think that, *cut it out.* Let people think what they think, just as long as they don't do anything to cause physical harm or danger to you or someone you know. It all boils down to you feel how you feel and they feel how they feel no one has to get rushed to the nearest hospital emergency room because you have a different ***perspective*** or view on things.

Yikes!

Gaining a ***perspective*** or point of view on things requires that you consider the facts, details, or maybe evidence before forming an opinion, response or reaction to anything.

One thing is certain, the older you get it will become extremely important for you to know and understand your ***purpose*** in life. You might be asking yourself "What is this thing called purpose?" Remember in the beginning of this book, you were reminded that you are part of a royal priesthood. You are brilliant in every spectacular way. You shine. You sparkle. You are your own bling. It's in your eyes, your walk, and even how you talk. You've got natural innate SWAG and didn't even know it.

At times, some of us have to get a little worn down for your *purpose* to actually shine its brightest. No worries, you're still here and you've made it. Now, it's time for you to figure out what you can offer the world to help someone else discover their **purpose**. You might also consider how you can work with others and how your skills and contributions ultimately help someone else, your community, or perhaps the world. These actions and thoughts drive this thing we call *PURPOSE*.

Think of it this way, everyone is here to meet a need of mankind. Your greatness, royalty, integrity, honesty, kindness, compassion, and love helps to protect the greatness of others... if you can understand that? Simply put, you are here to be incredible at whatever you do that can positively help, encourage, or assist someone else in Living their Best Life. Your **purpose**, aspirations, or mission in life is definitively *"not about you"*. It's more about your actions and how it magnifies, illuminates or enhances your royalty. It's usually a skill, gift, or ability that you are proud of, respected for, and can make good use of. In making good use of your **purpose**, you invariably create a good work. Never forget that your **purpose**, work, and deeds are always rooted in something that's good. Bottom line, if you're doing something that you're not exactly proud of, then it has absolutely nothing to do with the **purpose** that God has in mind for you.

Mastery of the **four P's** is sure to lend a perfect means to successfully coping with the challenging people and overwhelming situations that you may be dealt someday. An A+ effort in living your Best Life requires that you take time to think, analyze, and then ACT. Think before you act or respond to your circumstances. In today's world, you'd be surprised how many young and older people react or respond to things *without thinking*. Quick, snap reactions to someone who disrespected or offended you or someone you love. So, if you subscribe to the kiss and blow traditions of the hood, it is likely you will kiss, hug, and cry over the painful devastation brought when you refuse to consider the consequences of your snap responses, premature judgements, or dice throwing risks.

Check this out.

I love Danika Patrick. She is a retired award winning female NASCAR driver who is skilled with expert precision for driving cars at very high speeds. I always joke that *I trained Danika* to be as awesome as she is... taught her everything she knows. So not true. I wish. Yes, I'm just joking whenever I say that because I consider myself to be a pretty skilled driver. Yes, I am a skilled driver, but I'm no Danika. All this to say, as skilled as I think or know I am, I would never gamble or risk my life challenging another driver especially within city limits if there is the smallest chance that someone could be injured or worst. Never. I'm constantly thinking of others and how my actions could

possibly impact someone else Some might say, you are so Punky Brewster (1980's sitcom) for that. Noooooooo, that's so "I'm going home tonight and get in my bed. ...Don't have time for Grady Memorial Hospital". It's called weighing my odds and keeping a mature and leveled head in the driver's seat. Yes, I'm a very good driver. But I'm not a trained racecar driver. There is a difference. Danika has trained to do what she does well for countless years and days to be able to *maneuver* race cars at 200plus miles per hour. Come on folks I'm baaad, but I ain't crazy.

In life, we must take time to weigh the odds and consequences in everything that we do. It's important to assess dilemmas, predicaments, and problems just as you evaluate the road when you are driving. Before you make a decision to respond to whomever or whatever has triggered you, think about the people you care about and their expectations of you. *Think*. Think about your goals in life and how your response could potentially cancel whatever plans you have. Making it plain, I took the long road to stress the importance of <u>thinking</u> <u>before</u> <u>you</u> <u>react</u> to anything. *Think*. Stay calm and know that when you allow yourself to take a deep breathe you can effectively determine how important the other party is or is not.

After so many years of working with teenagers and young adults, I realized that some youth just don't want to take the time to **Prioritize**, put things and people into **Perspective**, and stay focused on discovering their **Purpose**. Some

almost refuse to do it and this is a recipe for disaster. It's true, you stifle and choke your royal tapestry when you don't protect it. Tap into your *NOAH*... that thing that gives you the capacity to know right from wrong and you feel it in your gut.

At the back of this book you will find pages to take notes, so please do. Take a few notes to describe what you want and need in your life. You can number these things from most important to the least important. It's perfectly okay to want things, but you should understand the difference between wants and needs. Just know that the latter tends to suggest that this is something you really can't live without. Now on the other side of this pendulum is something called wants and these are things that really won't make a difference in your life whether you have them or not.

The difference is seen in the maturity level of the individual when one makes these assessments and considers what makes sense and what doesn't. A mature thinking man or woman realizes that as soon as I have what I really need, I can then plan on "when" I can get what I want. Right here is where I'd like to offer a bonus P and that would be the word **Process**. It's just a good idea to *think* about things while trying to understand its formation, development, or progression in your life. It takes time to sort things out in our lives. So you're not alone if it's taking a minute. Process is just another fancy word for think, but just think on a deeper level.

In our western civilization, we respect **daily prayer** or meditation as that solemn time to truly connect with the Almighty God. At this time we give sincere thanks for having yet another day to walk in our purpose. If you're still not sure about your purpose, you can pray to ask God for wisdom or direction in understanding dilemmas or other challenges you might me having. Some will seek confirmation about their purpose or relationships in their life. **Prayer** is that time to beckon or engage the highest level of peace and calm in our lives. In this moment, you surrender everything that resembles a storm in your life. It's that time to seal the deal. You as an individual rest your hope, confidence, and trust in **BELIEVING** that the Almighty God has heard your petition and will do everything to help you realize success and indisputable victory! **Amen.**

Chapter 7:
Starting Off on the Wrong Foot

Young love. Right now I am thinking about this film from the 1970s called Aaron Loves Angela, released in 1975 starring Kevin Hooks and Irene Cara. This film is seen as an urban adaptation of Romeo and Juliet written by William Shakespeare. Well, Aaron and Angela lived in Harlem, New York. Aaron was a young black teenager and Angela was Puerto Rican. Fast forward, their relationship was seen as "interracial" and their parents did not approve of it. Like Romeo and Juliet, they continued to see each other anyway and eventually found themselves in the middle of a very violent and dangerous predicament when trying to defend their love.

Thank goodness our world has changed in many regards whereas people don't have to necessarily or literally fight for their love. People are free for the most part to pursue who they want and be with whom they want. I've heard a lot of stories about relationships and how they tend to unravel. Thinking about some of these tales, I thought it would be helpful to share a few treasured gems concerning young love and teenage courtship.

Oh-oh here I am dating myself again.

Over the years, I have noticed that there are many many people who never subscribe to the concept of courtship. Truth be told, both young and older people don't really believe in courtship or dating anymore. A lot of that rests in financial hardship and limited funds to regularly spend money going here, there, and everywhere. Funny thing is that I see true dating or courtship as a real friendship... **THAT'S BONA FIDE**.

What do platonic friends do anyway? Spend a lot of time on the phone and find things to do that are FREE or they go Dutch (whereas each person pays their own bill). Just spending time with someone you really enjoy being with can be a wonderful experience. They make you laugh and you can always find something to talk about. Chillin'. You can watch football, basketball and tennis together. Ole school folks enjoy playing cards and going to jazz clubs. They like movies and concerts too.

During one of our BONA FIDE teen talk sessions, my kids figured they would keep it 100 with me on the topic of dating in the new millennium. According to them, a large number of young people enjoy going to parties, movies, special events, and eating at buffet restaurants. Ya'll love to eat. In talking and doing a lot of listening I learned about hot boxing, smoke sessions in abandoned houses, the popularity of hotel parties, and Air BNB parties.

What-da-What is hot boxing?

Its smoking marijuana in a car with all its windows and doors closed to create a very smoky/foggy-space. I also learned about another popular craze using marijuana in which youngsters create edibles in the form of tasty treats such as: chocolate brownies, candy, cereal, cookies, lollipops, gummy bears, etc.

Wow, some of my millennials

are clearly doing the most and

waaaay too darn much of it.

I'm not sure where you are or where you live in the world but there have been news reports on American national television networks about the activities of middle and high school students using edibles. I was clueless until seeing the news reports. When I asked my students about the news reports I saw, they had plenty to share and plenty to confirm. Wow.

So, someone at a local middle school (junior high school grades 6-8) gave their classmates edibles and the students who ate the edibles became violently ill whereas EMS had to be called and other students were rushed to the hospital.

Who does that??????????

Again no-judgement, but this is a very serious situation. I'm just saying... As a young, healthy, thinking, and vibrant

person it's important that you consider the pros and cons of everything. There's a lot to be said about this entire scenario and an excellent time to really think about the roles of everyone involved in this event. If you think you need help getting your life on track, please reach out for help. For information purposes, please see the resource guide found in chapter 19.

Chapter 8:
What's Up?

On this particular day, one of my boys came in the room complaining about not having a girlfriend. He was very free and open about it. No one asked him any questions. No one in the group was talking, yet he felt compelled to seek attention for his frustrations. Of course, I always attempt to keep students on task with their work, but from time to time students will continue on with their side bar comments and light chatter.

What was interesting is how this student complained about how most girls treated him and that he always ends up the third wheel when he hangs out with friends who are dating. Let me preface this by sharing that this young man is hilarious. He is very funny. He has a natural comedic affect when talking and telling his truth. When he talks, he likes to stand up and plead his case in front of the entire class. So, he's hard to ignore. Based on so many of his comments at different times and on different days, the responses of his peers force me to either investigate further or get them to expound on their thoughts.

Over time, my precious millennials have told the truth about how they typically end their teenage relationships. Some admitted that it can be as simple as sending a mere text message, blocking a person's phone number, or doing

disrespectful acts in a very "loud" way to be seen on social media. Specifically, the dumped or duped individual can see their special friend booed-up with someone else...posted on social media for hundreds or perhaps thousands of eyeballs to see.

Social Media can be a BEAST.

When it comes to matters of the heart, it takes a mature person to take the high road. Meaning to *talk* to the individual you want to distance yourself from. Just work on telling-it-like-it is, but in the most respectful way imaginable. That's real talk for a grown person. At the end of the day, these text messages and blocked calls all spell out REJECTION at any grown folks table I sit at. As my students hear and debate about these breakup schemes, they agreed that the best way to let someone go or end a relationship is slowly but surely. So, ideally you should be ready to pace yourself with something like that. Can you do that? One thing is certain, if you can show that kind of consideration, you might certainly keep a *platonic* friend for life.

It was refreshing to learn that the millennials do also refrain from introducing new people to their family members whom they know the relationship won't lead to anything serious. On another day, students were talking about their serious relationships and how long it takes for them to *consummate* a relationship at their young ages.

This group of kids were wild and wide open.

Straight up random comments.

No Cap! Someone would say something completely off the wall and I would respond with

What da What??

Then another student would commence to bring me up-to-speed with where the comment originated. The kids always laughed as they tried to keep me clued in. Both girls and boys have talked quite freely about what attracts them to the opposite sex, what keeps someone around and how you end up on the <u>BLOCK list</u>.

Often, I would say… What?? What?? What you say?? Just as often as I would say, can you please cut all the side bar conversations?

I can still hear you. You know that I have bionic hearing.

…Get your work done.

When I first heard my student repeatedly saying "On Block." I chimed in with ... What?? You mean like Warren Campbell's... MY Block??

What da What?

Just me being goofy with my kids. Surprisingly, there were many students who reported that they use the call block method to end a relationship.

Yikes!! *Oh My.*

So, here is where I question my students, "What happens when you see this person in school? How do you deal with the discomfort, feelings of anger or perhaps uneasiness because you feel brushed off?"

That's deep.

These millennials are rough.

My goodness.

Another student candidly shared that he has no problem with putting a girl On Block and sometimes it can happen pretty fast. Sometime later, I eventually got around to sharing with this young man that *someday* he will meet a wonderful girl who is totally handling her business and also celibate aka abstinent and how would he conduct himself should that occasion happened or came to fruition. His response was simply this: "And she'll be On Block too, cause she won't be able to do nothing for me."

What-da-What???

Lord, Please Help the Children!

I told one of the men on faculty about some of the crazy things our boys are saying. I was interested in knowing if anyone had a chance to have real conversations with them about growing and maturing from boys to men? It's true, I'm no man and would never try to stand in a man's shoes but I couldn't help but remind my young boys that having multiple sexual partners is never a smart thing to do. No matter how many condoms you have in your pocket, it's still a ridiculous path to be on. Some students have earnestly shared that once you get started, if you *intentionally slow down or stop*, you might as well have stayed a virgin.

What da *What-What- What*???

Double Yikes!

Let me be clear, I do have some boys who are mature and are very respectful. These are my boys who say it's perfectly fine for both boys and girls to stay virgins until their 25 or 30 if that's what they choose to do. Bless God. I was so happy and proud to hear that they thought as I do that staying a virgin as long as you like is perfectly fine. More important is that when you are a teenager, having a girlfriend or boyfriend should be a fun experience without being overwhelmed with stress, pressure, or shaming. What alarmed me most were my boys that sat and made comments about their sexual escapades as though they were grown men. *NO CAP.*

As you can see, I am always concerned about what my students are thinking or doing and how their dare devil thinking informs their risky behavior. It goes beyond the unhealthy, unsafe, and risky decisions to have sex with as many people that say yes, but more about making choices that could potentially end your life.

Hearing young boys talk so cavalier about "smashing" girls pains me and it has made me wonder to what degree has this attitude been passed on from older generations.

Who do we blame for this?

This is the question of the day. No indictment for anyone or anything in particular. Just a question… who or what is at fault and how do we create the paradigm shift for our millennials and other generations to come? I firmly believe that talking is a great start. If there is no authentic or transparent engagement, then you have no idea what people are thinking and why they think what they think. We actually just keep going along, keep moving, keep doing, and keep being flabbergasted by the evening news. There is no doubt that there will be some to criticize that I allow my students to talk so freely. *I sure do.* There is also no doubt that I question them when I hear things that sound risky. It's very common for me to question… "What did you just say?" I maintain a very respectful environment and the kids know how to keep their comments appropriate. They know there's no judgement, so you hear exactly what they really-

really think. My kids/students also knew not to cross the line with disrespectful rants or use of any profanity. Must have zero tolerance for something.

The amazement is real!

At the end of the day, I often remind my students that school should be their first priority and that all other things come second, third, or fifty-five. If you're stressing about not being asked to the prom. Remember this famous mantra, Find a Way or Make a Way. Simply put, think of some positive options you can consider that will resolve your dilemma. For instance, can you go to the prom with a group of friends who also haven't found a date? Trust and believe, you are not the only person without a date. Perhaps you might consider going to the prom with a relative whom your classmates haven't met. There's always options that make sense.

Some young people become concerned about their looks and feeling unattractive. Yes, I respect and realize that some youth do struggle with their thoughts about self-image. Here is where I must remind you that "beauty is in the eye of the beholder". Know this, that everyone see's beauty or attractiveness on an individual basis. If you're not willing to allow people to make their own decisions, then it really sounds like you're trying to be the boss of someone else's thoughts. Please don't do that. The bottom line is that we sometimes are way too hard on ourselves and the very

thing that we think people are paying attention to, they never really noticed it until you started trippin' or being overly concerned about it. So stop wasting your time and start doing something you enjoy, have good fun and be intentional about living your Best life.

When you're having those growing- up pains, it's a good idea to find and connect with a mentor. A great mentor is someone you can discuss your questions and concerns about personal image with. Don't keep stressing about something you can work on or learn ways to change what you're not happy with. Talk with an adult you trust and you can explore ways to improve the things that are adding stress to your life.

Please understand this… anyone can "clean up" as they say. Truth is, when we begin to allow ourselves to become concerned about things that should be secondary in our lives, the primary things suffer. Just know that when you concentrate on the right things, the secondary things will somehow work itself out especially when you find an adult you trust and can help you with developing your **SWAG**.

Now that's what up!

Chapter 9:
Watch Out Cause You Bout to Get Played!

Hearing multiple stories about so many young girls who get tricked or duped into sharing their nude pictures with teenage boys was heart wrenching. The stories all sounded alike. Boy professes his love, girl takes very private pictures and happily fulfills her boyfriend's request to send provocative or sexually stimulating pictures...then, you know the rest. And the rest can virtually include being humiliated by the entire student body, getting suspended or possibly expelled for willfully participating in such a compromising, pornographic, obscene, and improper act. One of the most important things you must always remember is that if something has the potential to ruin your reputation if it was somehow exposed to anyone other than who intended, then, it's not worth it, because you never know.

BONA FIDE talk alert: Any young man who ask you to send nude photographs does not respect you. Period. They don't even really like you. Think about it. Would they like it if someone dared to ask their momma, sister, auntie, or cousin that foolishness? Absolutely Not! So why is he asking you?

"...Girl, he tried you."

And you easily complied. So now that you're reading this book, you won't ever do that again.

Here's how you test your boyfriend who might ask you to send, text, or email a nude picture... all you have to do is ask this question: How would you like it if someone asked your Mom that?? If he reacts with disgust or anger, he's pissed and appalled that you would ask that. Good. So he won't be upset if you told him NO!

When a young man truly cares about his girl, lady, or boo... he takes pride in showing her how much he values her. He enjoys seeing her happy. He becomes very protective and will often warn you against things that aren't wholesome or pure in a sense. Umm hmm. That's just a young man who wants to protect what he sees as truly his and doesn't want anyone else to ever get the opportunity to shame or embarrass you. When you feel embarrassed, he feels embarrassed. So, he'd never pull that stunt with someone he treasures. Carefully *think* things out before you jump to do it... please. You'll be so proud of yourself when you do.

Think it out- Before you walk it out.

My best advice... **DON'T GET FINESSED!** Keep all things that are precious in a private and highly classified space.

Listen princess, you've got to respect yourself first before anyone else does. And if anyone dares to ever dull your

shine, just politely remind them of your royalty. It's okay to be honest and let boys know that you would never disrespect yourself like that and you wouldn't dare trust him to not group share your erotic and risqué photos. Yes, this is definitely an indecent proposal. Lastly, please remember that these kinds of provocative photos are illegal. It is a crime. If you willingly send these kinds of pictures, it means you are in some way an accessory to a crime.

SO, DON'T DO IT!

Oh yeah...It's also called child pornography. There are so many things that we must stay highly aware of. There is no time to play the "I didn't know card", that's why you're reading this book.

BONA FIDE TRUTH.

Never forget... that you are being tested when you are propositioned with things like this. Some boys will be aggressive or very persistent about making these kinds of requests. It's true, you're being tested and he's trying to determine just how far he can go with you. This tear-jerking onion continues to peel down to the fact that young men who make this kind of request are not only on a mission to publicly dishonor and disgrace you, but to get the heartiest laughs ever at your expense. Trust and believe regardless of how stunningly beautiful you may be... boys

will laugh and scream until tears fall over your huge *lapse in judgement*.

You will be the talk of the town. Kids may even point and whisper over the entire incident. ...But YOU trusted him. Indeed, it is very unfortunate that girls who make these snap decisions find themselves starring in the latest school gossip drama completely blinded to the fact that young boys are notorious for using things like this to get laughs, street cred and popularity.

THANK GOD

YOU KNOW BETTER NOW...

SO YOU CAN DO BETTER.

Don't forget that social media is now a part of normal everyday life for almost every age group in North America. Some kids like to post pictures on some of the biggest social media platforms around. Many popular kids have pages and pages on multiple platforms and will at times post a lot of inappropriate things with their selfies, nude pictures, or video footage of young and older women being degraded in some shape, form, or fashion. Teens admit that posting a fight is just as popular or acceptable as posting inappropriate pictures.

SO PLEASE STAY WOKE!!

Chapter 10:
Sparring for Attention

As much as my students talked about practically everything, I often felt the urge to say… What da What??

I also asked them hard questions too. I wanted to know, why do our kids fight so much? Why are certain kids literally a ticking-time-bomb if you happen to say good morning the wrong way? Although I already had my ideas, eyewitness accounts, the research, and other receipts to confirm what I was thinking, I appreciated hearing *exactly* what my millennials had to say…

Numerous students shared that sometimes the school fights are *inevitable* especially when a student who is being bullied feels that he or she has no other recourse to deal with the trauma of being bullied by a classmate. Regrettably, there are many who feel that fighting is the only way to retaliate against an aggressive perpetrator.

Some kids went on to report that a few bullies use such tactics as "bumper cars" or publicly throwing insults to an unsuspecting person. Bumper cars visually resemble when someone uses their body and or shoulders to aggressively push themselves into another unsuspecting person. When the innocent person is bumped, they are usually made to spill something, fall down, or become embarrassed in front

of other classmates. Again, to save face, it's a normal reaction to get up and want to fight the person who assaulted you for no apparent reason. Yes, it becomes very hard to not want to snatch a wig back when you've been embarrassed, humiliated, and laughed at. It's true that all of the above are very hard things to have to bargain within the corridors of our narrow hallways in a few of these schools across America today. It's tough out here in some of these streetz and schoolz people!

Peer Pressure is real

BONA FIDE... 1000

I heard students when they talked about the "bumper car" stories and how difficult it can be to defend yourself against mean girls and boys. Regrettably, it is often an unavoidable evil to not be engaged in a fight in order to protect your reputation when things like this happen within the crowded corridors of a neighborhood high school. Loud and clear I heard students who said that they really appreciate school cultures that have <u>zero tolerance</u> behavior policies, swift responses, and lightning consequences for students who instigate violence in our schools. As I have often said... please share important things like potential fights, acts of violence, and other infractions with a trusted adult at your school. This is definitely one of the most mature things you could ever do. Besides, it keeps the playing field safe for everyone, including you. And don't worry about being seen

as a snitch. A real BOSS knows how to handle getting tips about serious things without putting anyone in danger or on the spot. **No Cap**... find someone you trust to share serious information with at school. Believe me, you won't regret it.

According to the kids, the history of school fights actually has its origin in the neighborhoods of the students who find themselves suspended for doing mean things at its most dangerous levels. Many students talked over one another as they testified about being picked on and forced to fight in their neighborhoods. Story after story of kids sharing their testimonies of how fighting is something you had to do to prove to others that you could defend yourself if you needed to. ...So you were *trained* in your own back yard. "That's how the hood do it!" One student informed me. "Every time you go outside you have to fight because they make fun of you if you don't know how to defend yourself. That's how older boys and some grown men try to toughen you up," said another student.

It's **BONA FIDE** to say that many youngsters take pride in fighting and like to encourage others to archive their not-so-professional boxing matches. Somehow as mentioned earlier, a few of these brawls end up being seen by countless people on social media and network television. Well, if you engage in these assault antics please understand that you are flirting with a criminal offense that can get you a battery charge. When an unbridled teenager raises his arms with clenched fist and bald knuckles to

assault another person they are gambling their freedom and their education. Yes, I'll wait while you count all the days of out of school suspensions that take place on school campuses across this country due to school fights. Simply put, it has become a phenomenon in urban schools and it's not that rare either. On the contrary, it has become a somewhat common experience amongst youngsters who never take time to talk, understand, or listen. So, I wanted to take time to seriously consider these incidents and what more can be done to eradicate or at least further decrease school suspensions and dropout rates.

While trying to find the answers, it became clear that the teenage years are one of the toughest times for both boys and girls. It is a transitional phase between not being a child anymore but not yet being mature enough to be called an adult. Countless youth go through mental, physical, and emotional challenges during this time and this is also a time when they are prone to getting into trouble. Research indicates that approximately 1.1 million juvenile delinquency cases were filed against teenagers in 2013 alone.

For the purpose of helping us to understand how to neutralize this phenomenon, I wanted to share the common causes of the anger that erupts when the "bows" start flying in the cafeteria, classroom, and school hallway. Most teens and young adults are emotionally unstable. Period. It's called growing up. Typically, teenagers tend to have issues

with everyone, including their parents, peers, siblings, and sometimes their community. It's important for me to add that some teens and young adults do adopt physical aggression as a coping mechanism for very serious things that they have been left to deal with at a very young age. The gamut is wide as there are so many youth who reportedly experience physical abuse, neglect, homelessness, and many other things that have a tremendous impact on their young minds, innocence, and personal belief systems.

While we take a look at some of the main reasons why teenagers exhibit anger and sometimes resentment, research suggest that gaining individuality and independence are the primary culprits. And although children are fighting for independence everyday beyond infancy, teen years are the final years many are compelled to fight for their identity and independence. Another survey showed that 95% of teens have felt inferior about themselves at some point of their teen years.

Unfortunately, being a teenager at times can be such an overwhelmingly emotional time for youth that numbers of teens handle their emotional roller coaster through physical altercations with peers, verbal arguments with parents, and sometimes emotional melt downs with close friends. Other studies have shown that it is hormonal and bodily changes that can explain some of the inappropriate behavior exhibited by many teenagers. However, understanding the

difference between right and wrong is still a reasonable expectation.

Another reason why teenagers can sometimes exhibit aggression or anger is because of their bodily changes. Teenage years are one of the worst times of an individual as far as appearance is concerned because while the body hasn't yet fully matured, it's no longer the same as a child's. Because of this, teenagers become self-conscious about their skin, hair, complexion, and a range of other features.

A study done in 2010 showed that children in mid to late stages of puberty exhibit three times more violence and aggression as compared to those that had just entered their teenage years. While arguments and experimentation with alcohol or drugs is a normal part of the growing process, there are a few serious complications that both teenagers and parents need to be aware of.

Research conducted in 2014 showed that while all teenagers had experienced anger, 50% regretted their emotion and actions. 7.1% of teenagers had hit another person during their burst of anger and 25% had resorted to hitting a nearby object. Excessive fighting, bullying, or any other form of physical violence is a sign you should watch out for. Bullying is an outward form of expressing anger and this is why young adults should be taught how to control the emotion instead of expressing it in a negative way.

According to statistics, 50% of teens have misused drugs at least once in their lives. Causes behind drug and alcohol abuse include insufficient brain development, curiosity, peer pressure, anger, and emotional struggles. Due to alcohol and substance abuse, teens may get into legal trouble and end up in jail. Reckless driving, illegal activities, and fighting with peers may cause teens to be trapped in juvenile delinquency cases.

Youth I hear you when you confide that some parents of teens are at times helpless when it comes to managing their child's mental health and emotional instability. While it is true that all teens will go through emotional changes during adolescence, parent reactions can help teens to control their anger. Anger management issues are common in teenagers. A number of studies indicate that a number of problems and incidents have gone by without interventions. However, if you think things are getting out of control at your school, you should always reach out for help by talking with a trusted adult or your parent.

Chapter 11:
Mad at the Whole World...

Managing anger is an emotion that has been found to be one of the hardest things for today's teenagers to grapple with. As an educator for more than 20 years, I have heard about and also witnessed some of the most brutal waltzes one could ever imagine. No, our students weren't dancing, but I wish they were. Instead they were exchanging blows as though each fighter had a professional title to defend. Brutal and sometimes bloody. Unfortunately, both the girls and boys fight.

Nowadays you just might catch a glimpse of the latest school fight on your evening news due to someone posting the event on social media. "Did you see us on Facebook, Instagram, or YouTube?" someone would question the next day. Students confide that fighting and the enjoyment of seeing it as a free spectator sport is yet another folly that is widely acceptable amongst both middle and high school students. Teenagers admit that watching school fights have become something popular for people to *increase their popularity* in school and on social media platforms winning them thousands of followers.

Teens continue to confess that those who grow massive numbers of followers are typically posting things like fights, photos of them flashing money, having cars, and

promoting their businesses. Yes, these junior entrepreneurs aka millennials have become ingenuous as they make hundreds and sometimes thousands of dollars online selling their clothes, shoes, tattoo art, and crack house fruit made with crushed candy or cool-aid. Unknown to me until now, there are other young adults who are going so far as to sell outrageous things with just a simple purchase using the golden cash app. Thank God none of my students were known to do that, but they are very aware of those who push the limits selling all kinds of things on social media.

WHOA!!

What-da What??

The only thing I can offer from my heart is...

If you want help finding ways to deal with your feelings of anger, please talk with a trusted adult. You can also consult with a variety of agencies that provide counseling or coaching services to help you gain better control over your life. Realizing that it's time to explore some alternatives to losing your temper, hurting others, or getting yourself into trouble is a pretty good idea. When you're ready, please look at the resource guide at the back of this book. This guide is provided to give you a directory of contact information for all kinds of trained professionals whom you can talk with.

I'm all about keeping the conversations going. So, keep the conversations going by talking about what's really keeping you upset or perhaps unhinged?

Bonafide Talk...

what's keeping you disturbed and mad so much that it disrupts your life on a consistent basis?

This is something you should take time to think about.

There are a lot of questions you can begin to think about. Questions along with honest answers are needed to better understand YOURSELF and the challenges you face. This kind of processing or introspection is necessary for learning how to control your feelings and emotions. Think about it. When you get into *"Your Feelings"*, how does a situation work out for you? If you're honest about it, things usually don't turn out so great.

I was going to list a bunch of great questions here for you to think about and write the answers to them... but I'm not. Instead, I am encouraging you to talk with someone and allow that person to ask you questions so that you can create a strong dialogue around your answers, *your truth*, and your feelings about whatever it is that compromises your success.

Please check out the resource guide and find someone you can talk with. There is a caring professional who can help

you sort it all out. Accepting help from a trained professional will help you to get your life on the right track. Protect your *royalty*, if you're not able to connect with a professional counselor, therapist, or life coach, remember that you can always find help with a trusted mentor, teacher, or perhaps minister. Your life will change for the better when you talk more about what's aggravating you.

In addition to talking with someone you trust, consider doing the things that help you to avoid getting upset, such as listening to music, walking, jogging, riding a bike, watching a great movie, or visiting a good friend. You decide, just as long as you're doing something that makes you feel relaxed and peaceful. Be intentional about doing things that can help you to stay in control of yourself and your destiny.

#When you control yourself, you remove the opportunity for someone or something else to control you.

NO CAP!

Chapter 12:
Esteem in Me

Developmentally, we know that teenagers and young adults have arrived to the age of wanting to do everything themselves. You want to make your own decisions without the direction or input of most adults that you know, especially your parents. Since you have made up your mind that you want to do it all by yourself, you invariably open yourself to making mistakes. Some mistakes are reversible, and some are not. Just as you fight to have your voice and opinions heard, researchers suggest that this is that time when teens and young adults want to face their biggest challenges in life without the help of anyone outside of their generation. It appears that at this age, some youth actually believe that they are "grown" when they realistically aren't quite there yet.

Scholars have suggested that every individual is not only the product of their own family but also of their community or society at large. Teenagers absorb things like a human sponge not only from his or her own house but also from their neighborhood. The external variables which tend to have the most influence with teenagers will include their friends, classmates, teachers, and other acquaintances. I was interested in the phenomenon of television and its impact on juveniles back in the 1980's. Almost two decades later, there are mountains of evidence that reveal

some level of influence from our twenty-first century television content, music, movies, and yes, social media.

Our millennials typically do a lot of good and bad things all decided upon by themselves. Yes, youth often make executive decisions about life without the knowledge of their parents or another caring adult. In such instances, parents may get a phone call from a concerned teacher or school administrator. If a child's school has not given a parent a heads-up to check on their student, then a worst case scenario might involve the local police department calling home to have parents come to their local precinct to pick up their teenager. In these instances, parents often become the fall guy.

Many are quick to blame the parent, when in fact the child made their own "executive" decisions without consulting with anyone older than 16 or 17. Although guardians are responsible for "raising" their children, I believe its good when a level headed adult can assist their teenager in his or her successful transition through early, middle, and late adolescence. Teenagers do a lot to avoid the input of their parents or other adults they know, I believe it's a good idea when a levelheaded adult can assist any teenager in passing the milestones of growing into full adulthood. Case in point, I am known to joke with younger adult friends saying things like: "I know you're grown, but you're not yet good & grown". This suggest that as we grow older,

there is a lot of wisdom to be shared due to the years of life experiences we have.

Honestly, if you want a smooth transition through adolescence to your teens and then to your adult life, find a great adult that can tell you something about how to successfully grow older.

Across the span of years starting at the early teens and lasting well into your early twenties, youth are battling to make perfect sense of the physical, sexual, social, cognitive, and emotional changes you are experiencing. You want to feel confident and would prefer to keep a positive outlook on life. I believe that talking will help you understand what you're feeling. Depending on who your talking with, you ay be able able to gauge how many others feel the same way that you do.

As teenagers and young adults learn to constantly adjust their personal plans, outlook, decisions, and self- approval, many are tormented with having low self-esteem. Author Brian Tracy defines self-esteem as having confidence in your own self-worth, ability to complete various task, having self-respect, and assertiveness. He and other researchers agree that your self-esteem can improve over time. However, as you work hard to gain more confidence, it is important to have pride, dignity, and faith in yourself.

As it relates to your ability to succeed in so many of the conquest and adventures you are certain to have in your

adult life, it is important to have the self-esteem, drive, tenacity, and fortitude to complete whatever you aspire to do in life. At the end of the day, you must lick that element of stick-to-it-ti-venous in order to accomplish anything that is worthwhile or worth having.

Does that sound corny? Maybe it does... but it's important to have these things if you want to experience life at its fullest.

NO CAP!

I hope you have been able to see that your life can be exactly what you want it to be. If you just take time to advance and pull your skills up in the different areas mentioned throughout this book, you'll be just fine.

Having as many conversations as possible about your determination and commitment to setting and accomplishing smart and reasonable goals is a great way to start improving your self-esteem. Take one step at a time. Concentrate on something you can be successful at doing when you put energy and effort into realizing your goal. Building your self-esteem most certainly requires that you adopt the spirit of the lion who is known to be strong, determined, and tough. Be firm about what it is that you want to accomplish. You can do it. Don't be afraid to walk in your truth. Most important, never be too proud to find others who can help you achieve what you desire to do in your life.

Finding a positive person, like a family member, mentor, or friend who believes in you can only make accomplishing your goal that much sweeter. Start today by outlining a plan for reaching at least 2 or 3 ambitions you've set for your future.

Chapter 13:
Where Did This Low Self-Esteem Stuff Come From Anyway...

The truth of the matter is, what seem insignificant to adults might be the very things that may cause a teenager's self-esteem to take a dive. What's important to remember is that it could be a wide variety of things, including concerns about acne, extra body weight, a break up with a significant other, or perhaps a unintentional comment made by an adult you look up to. If you've had a dip in your self-esteem, it's nothing to really worry about. If you ever get into a place where you can't seem to bounce back within a reasonable period of time, then please find help. Find an adult you trust to just talk to. Chop it up. Get a trusted adult's feedback on what you're thinking and feeling.

If you are under the age of 22, please understand that your self-esteem and confidence are very important to your growth and development. Strides towards you becoming a mature, positive, and balanced individual hinges upon how you feel about yourself. Your self-esteem is so critical that if you ever begin to feel down and start believing negative thoughts about yourself, it is likely to create a domino effect of adverse feelings that may create a downfall in your life.

How will you know if you need to check your self-esteem thermostat? For beginners, pay attention to the times you experience feelings related to an inability to experience success in school. Be real about the times you find it hard to concentrate on your class work. Be honest about the times it becomes very hard to eliminate thoughts that make it easy for you to stay distracted or distressed. If you were once very active and involved in sports or other extra-curricular activities then suddenly lose interest in the things you enjoyed most at school, it's a good time to change the game or talk about what you can do to find other positive interest.

Attraction to social illness, danger, high risk, jeopardy, and peril become intriguing and attractive to many youth who lose their self-esteem. Here is where we see considerable involvement in social illness by youth who lack confidence in their class work, sports, peer relationships, or anything that is important to them. If you're wondering where that word social illness came from, some have referred to community violence and mayhem as a social illness. Albeit, some of my students may be living and/or existing in rough and rugged neighborhoods, many find constructive ways to remain resilient, strong, and determined to keep it pushing. Through it all, it's important that you understand that total wellness is possible.

Real Talk... right before our eyes on the evening news we can regularly see countless young people accepting their

fate which is dealt by the very deeds they commit or offer themselves to. Although many teens who struggle with poor self-esteem and low self-confidence find themselves involved in unhealthy and dangerous exploits, all is not lost.

If you are a teenager or perhaps an individual who hasn't turned 25 yet, but you have surrendered to such frequent activities as smoking, drinking, drug use, promiscuity, chronic school absences, or perhaps school dropout, you could be on a slippery slope to somewhere you ultimately don't want to be. **No CAP** all these things I just mentioned could be indicative of someone who truly needs help. Someone who really wants help. I can't stress this fact enough that improving your self confidence and self-esteem can happen.

If you haven't found yourself a good mentor, PLEASE find that trusted adult so you can TALK. Talk-It-Out. Usually, there will be no limit to the topics you can speak about. You might want to talk about your self-image and things you can do to improve your looks or school performance.

You might be that young person who has overbearing parents who are more than capable of supervising and raising you. Just know that these parents have the best intentions and only want what's best for you and don't ever forget that. Just know that if you're feeling less than confident that you can do anything to please your parents or any other family member or make them happy, consider

having a conversation with them. That's right show the "maturity" in you by gently broaching this topic with them. If you feel that would be next to impossible to do, then always make the attempt to discuss your feelings with a trusted adult.

Lastly, I want you to think about joining at least one or more school activities as this can be a perfect way to connect with other students who enjoy the same things you enjoy or have similar aspirations. Yes, clubs can be a very good thing. However, don't forget that you may encounter peers who aren't as supportive, friendly, or helpful. No worries. It can still be worth your time because you may meet a new friend or two while you participate in activities that are fun, fulfilling, and enjoyable.

Ultimately, there is no magic potion that anyone can take to feel good about themselves, to feel self-assured, and tenacious about accomplishing something worthwhile in life. You must understand that there is absolutely no hypnotic tonic that would add a sizable measure of self-esteem in any teenager. Having the heart to be more courageous and bolder about making smart decisions for your life takes planning.

Plan it out…

before you walk it out.

That's what thinking people do.

Chapter 14:
MENTORS...What's the Big Idea?

Bob Proctor said it this way "A mentor is someone who sees more talent and ability within you, than you see in yourself, and helps bring it out of you."

Mentors are the people you can talk to who can offer you different perspectives in life. They can help you with developing plans, goals, and understanding the how and why we look at things the way that we do. A trusted mentor is the perfect person to share your thoughts with and hear other perspectives on issues or circumstances you may be dealing with.

Your mentors will often last a lifetime. So if you don't have a mentor, try to find one. They are great for helping us to understand our truths and why we feel the way we do. If you don't have a mentor, it is strongly recommended that you find that special person. A mentor will typically be an adult that you respect and feel a connection with. At times, your mentor will be an adult that has the career you'd like to have someday.

When teenagers and other students find a great mentor, it is often someone who fills a role at school such as a coach, teacher, perhaps guidance counselor or academic advisor. If you haven't had the opportunity to connect with someone

who has the career you're interested in, you should consider recruiting another adult at your school. Keep this in mind, a mentor will typically be an adult whom you respect and enjoy discussing different topics with.

Most importantly, this is a person you trust and have great confidence that he or she has your best interest or Best Life in mind when offering you any advice. They only want the best for you and remind you of that often. Finally, mentors tend to be great sounding board or incredible listeners who are always ready to give you feedback whenever you ask. They are true diamonds to have in our lives. You will learn a lot from your mentor.

You Can Never Lose With a Great Mentor.

All youth need caring adults in their lives. Although positive and constant relationships with parents speak for a critical part of a teenagers life, other adults can provide guidance that is similar to the support a parent gives. The support provided by other adults can either be in addition to that provided by a parent or in place of support that a parent neglects to provide or is unable to give.

If you don't have a mentor, you should know that a trusted mentor can play a huge part in helping you to develop your self-esteem and confidence to do things that will enrich your life tremendously. Some young people benefit from their mentors who help them with their behavior and gaining or keeping self-control.

Being a part of the millennial generation is exciting. You and your peers were born ready to take over, run and literally rule the world. In many regards, it hasn't taken you long to figure out how to effectively influence others. If you have an interest in business, the arts, sports, or anything that requires explosive numbers to help you to succeed, many in your generation have proven that you have the Midas touch. You are a creative and cutting edge people. The adults who raise you, coach you, counsel you, teach you, and work with you understand the dynamic energy many of you have.

Keeping that energy from bursting or spilling aimlessly is what a mentor can help you with. No Cap, you will grow to treasure your mentor. The right mentor will become invaluable to your life. These are the trusted adults who are available to give you great feedback, advice, guidance, recommendations, and emotional support.

Your mentor can also provide you a good outlet if you ever need to discuss something that would be difficult to do with your parents. Many people will admit that their mentors have had a tremendous impact on their life especially in the absence of one or both parents. If you haven't been fortunate enough to find a mentor at school, you can think about connecting with someone at your church, there are also mentoring programs in your community (i.e. Boys & Girls Clubs, YMCA, and other community based organizations that have programs for youth).

Listen, if you know you can benefit from a positive person providing you with frequent motivation to get you up, going, moving, and doing... take the time to find that person who can help keep your self-esteem and confidence lifted. They are your personal cheer leaders. The relationship you develop with your mentor can provide you with a platform to truly understand the dynamics of establishing a trusting relationship with adults who are not in your immediate family.

Over time, I've realized that there are a lot of young people who do not have mentors. At the end of the day, your mentor is there to help you grow, mature, and understand a long list of things that you are sure to experience in your young life. Some mentors can be extremely helpful in you making improvements with your behavior, academics, and meeting goals you've set. Other mentors assist young adults with eliminating or reducing harmful or at-risk behavior. There are mentoring programs that run the gamut. Again, some mentoring programs can be found at your school or in your community.

Chapter 15:
Don't Forget to Dream

What was your last dream? Do you remember it? Perhaps you daydreamed about your life after high school, after college or life after you survive whatever you might be going through right now. You will survive.

I recently asked a young man who is graduating in a matter of weeks if he could share any words of wisdom with the students he will leave behind, he said to tell you "To always remember to learn from other people's mistakes along with your own mistakes". I thought that was so profound. It makes sense because we all make mistakes, the list of honest mistakes we can make in a life time can reach as far as the Amazon River... and that's pretty long. As long as you're learning and changing with each mistake... it's okay. It's really okay.

"Stay focused, go after your dreams

and keep moving towards your goals."

LL Cool J.

I remember saying earlier that you must identify your goals in life. Your goals are snap shots of your dreams. Do you have your list? What do you need to stay focused on? Peter

Raeth (Informationanthology.net, 2008) says that the first step to creating a goal is to have a clear vision of your dreams. That makes sense to me. Honestly, I believe that's exactly what it is. So, I wanted to see if there was anyone who agrees with me. ...And there is.

Yes, we dream something or gain a strong desire for something and then we set goals to realize or DO IT. Plain and simple. If you dream of being at the top of your game, whatever that is. Then it only makes sense that you invest a lot of time cultivating, preparing, developing, and improving what you want to be known for. It makes sense that you would set goals for yourself that would invariable help or assist you with "living" the dream you have. So, if you want to live your dream, you should definitely carve out enough time to complete the tasks that will keep you on the road to your best life.

When I think of a Best Life Highway, I envision many opportunities that are simply a blessing from God. Honestly, they are things that would enable you to use whatever gifts, skills, or strengths you have to **IMPACT** whomever God needs you to be available for. When you truly think about it, that's the golden key to living our best life. Our Best Life really has nothing to do with us. Imagine that. Your Best Life is ushered in when you can help someone else have their Best Life experience. Explaining it like that, somehow we know that it's all reciprocal.

As you consider developing a list of things you can do to get focused on goals that can urge your dreams to manifest, here are a few things you might consider adding to your list:

1) Start your day with a prayer or meditation. Take at least 5 or 10 minutes to sit quietly. As you sit quietly think about your most creative, innovative, or ingenious ideas that connects you to your dream. Then, consider the goals you've set for that day and how you will successfully complete your goals for the day.

2) Using the present tense, create a personal affirmation or truth about yourself. This is something you should memorize and recite each day. An affirmation is similar to making a mission statement for yourself. It is a true statement which describes who you are now or affirms who you are becoming. Powerful stuff!

3) Try putting positive music in your ears. No doubt, I love all kinds of music including rap/ hip hop and R&B. However, much more than that, I love gospel music.

It's true, I listen to everything.

I listen to old school gospel hits from well-known choirs, gospel groups, and individual recording artist on a daily basis. Music honestly helps me to constantly praise, worship, and honor God pretty often. Now... remember that I spent reasonable time developing talent and working

with recording artist that did not sing gospel. Therefore, I listen to all genres of music. ALL. If the talent is pretty obvious, as a consumer I can enjoy it when I hear it and not try to live it. I think my age and level of maturity allows me to avoid making the music lines gray. There are so many great gospel artist out today. At the end of the day, you should listen to music that is soothing and creates a *positive atmosphere* for **you** to think, reflect, and consider reasonable changes you might want to make in your life. Jazz is another great genre of music to consider listening to when you want to stay in a positive space.

The most important thing is that you understand that there is motivational and inspirational music created to propel and encourage you to live a life of abundance and triumph. There are tons and tons of music you can listen to that will help keep you focused on accomplishing your goals. So, listen to *whatever* brings you *positive* energy, thoughts, and concrete ideas for moving your life forward. **Just keep the music positive and that will be a huge help.**

4) Now that you've found positive music to listen to, connect yourself to the **positive people** you know. You need as much positive energy as you can get. Now this might be a good time to separate yourself from those you know who aren't so positive. You know... the drama seekers. Those who love to get an environment *turnt up* without the music. ... Not good. Are these people a necessary equation for you to reach your goal?

You decide.

5) Look at your personal To Do list and figure out what you can get done today. I'm sure you figured out a few things you must do to accomplish your goals, first, second, and third. So pick up where you left off. Just resolve to get it all done. Today might be the day you make phone calls, visit your mentor, fill out applications, and contact an old teacher or family member. Just check your list and do something.

6) Get into the habit of reading the local newspaper wherever you live. It's always good to stay abreast of what's going on in the world. It's the adult thing to do. Grown people talk about what's happening in our world. They also tend to know what's going on in places all across the world and not just in our immediate neighborhoods.

7) Stay organized and keep your eyes on the prize. Doing things that are directly related to accomplishing your goal will no doubt keep you focused on it.

8) You might consider sharing your personal goals with someone you trust so that this person can check on you and perhaps give you support and encouragement when you really need it. Sometimes, it really does work to know that there is someone who can help you remain accountable to your personal endeavor. Research has called these people in our lives "accountability partners".

9) I am a huge fan of vision boards. Some people have classes and also parties for this. People of all ages create their vision board. This collection or collage of photographs, pictures, and words are used to give credence and legitimacy to our vision or the dreams we have. Vision boards are so awesome. This board is often created out of cork or perhaps poster board. Any material that you can use to create a visual of your goals is the main idea here. People have used vision boards to display positive affirmations and quotes, their individual goals written down, and personal photographs. Vision boards are so huge that there are software, blogs, and news articles you can find to help you get started with it (www.huffpost.com 2015)

10) Always celebrate the successes of the day before. You deserve it. At times, you may fall off track and not do exactly what you set out to do, but you should celebrate when you have accomplished what you've had a vision of doing on a regular basis.

Chapter 16:
Ready-To-Go-Get-It

After several years of working in the entertainment industry by default I found that I really enjoyed working with adolescents and teenagers. Early on, many hours of sleepless nights were spent dreaming up some of the most innovative and forward thinking ideas that many had not even considered. Some call it being ahead of your time... that's what many will call you when you're under 30 and considered still green or not ripe or seasoned in a profession.. Managing recording artist and developing their brands was something I enjoyed and was often consulted about different ideas that would increase the visibility and sales of someone who wanted to sell an incredible amount of CD's. When you have big ideas and a lot energy, you might decide you want to run your company, just like myself. While developing brands for a few artists in New York and New Jersey, I started an artist management company. Eventually I went financially bankrupt trying to do that independently. Interestingly enough, at the same time this was happening, my former colleague Sean Puffy Combs was blazing a path straight to the top of entertainment heaven. It was also at that time when I worked on different projects with such artist as Jeff Redd, Mary J. Blige, and Jodeci. At that time, these artist were signed to Uptown/MCA Records.

This was the absolute ground floor of their world-renowned careers. All of the thanks and credit goes to my mentor, Terrie Williams, for helping to open those doors and pushing me to use the skills and talent that she always saw in me.

Caught up in the world-wind of trying to keep an entertainment management company afloat while taking on independent projects at different record companies, I somehow started substitute teaching. Needless to say, I truly enjoyed the days I accepted jobs as a substitute teacher and the rest is history. Once I made a firm decision to completely switch gears and continue my education in Atlanta, Georgia I became interested in working with students in public schools and juvenile detention settings. So, it makes sense that I've acquired solid experience as a mental health counselor, school social worker, teacher, principal, and school leader. However, the vast majority of my experience has been in teaching high school students.

Initially, upon meeting some of my students they were so undisciplined and unbridled. Yep, they tried me a few times. However, in a short period of time, they started listening to me, being respectful, willing to cooperate, and available to get serious about learning and showing me what they knew.

I've even had other students who were *turnt up* and stayed *turnt up* everywhere else in the school *but* in my classroom. Those babies were lit 24-7.

"How do you do that??"

"What da What??"

"Wow."

Yes, I've had those students whom I would *play*-threaten to put them in a headlock if they didn't *get-it-together*. I would also fuss like a momma or auntie would. Unfortunately, one student who I had to fuss at a lot was murdered a few short months after the last time I saw him in school. I was so heart broken. That's the student who always wanted to hug me and I would have to shoo him off to class. *Wow.*

In the early years, I worked with juvenile offenders of all ages and I loved it. I was completely fascinated and intrigued with all of the brilliant minds in front of me each day. Believe it, I have heard some <u>incredible</u> stories. Ultimately, I was convinced that "if" these young people would've taken a Na-nu Na-nu second *(Mork and Mindy 1970's sitcom)* to reconsider their actions or reactions to people or circumstances that they wouldn't have made a losing wager on their life and freedom. Adopting practical ways of thinking and "being" is sure to add years to your life and even more time to enjoy *Your Best Life.*

Well, if you're reading this book, it's safe to say that you're ready to *Get-Your-Best-Life*. You are now ready to show the world that you can make it on your own and live a life free from court appearances, fines, jail time, or evading the police. You are ready. You are ready to escape or avoid the snares of the street life. You can do it. You're stronger now and ready to show the world how to survive the 501 things that can turn you into a sex addict, predator, drug addict, alcoholic, booster, purse snatcher, drug dealer, drug runner, scam artist, computer hacker, computer fraud criminal, shoplifter, bully, thief, or a violent weapon wielding perpetrator.

Chapter 17:
Are You Ready?

Whenever you feel forced to do something dangerous, risky, or unhealthy to yourself or to others, it is time to get help. Help comes in so many forms. You can gain clarity, inspiration, love, and truth from a wide variety of people. The list is long, but it looks like this: loving parents, grandparents, aunts, uncles, God parents, cousins, neighbors, teachers, school administrators, coaches, doctors, or health clinicians. Help can also come from your pastor or other trusted clergy. People are here to help, so don't give up on finding an adult you TRUST.

Any caring and mature adult who is available to listen to you, give you sound advice, and assist you in developing a plan of action to reach your **Best Life** is worth recruiting for your **Life Readiness Team**. Depending on your individual circumstances, you will want a team of supportive people who can help keep you on the right path. You will know who is right for you based on the connection you are able to make with this individual.

Ultimately, just be ever so careful that the individuals you recruit are people of integrity, honor, optimism, and positivity. Plain and simple, if the person never smiles or laughs out loud, run for the hills ... because that's not what you need at this time. *You gotta laugh people.* Laughter

adds years to your life. Believe it. I do. I laugh or smile all the time. It keeps me upbeat, young, and happy. I love people who are funny. I have a lot of happy and funny people in my own family. They are a hoot!

Bottom line, if you say something funny, I will laugh.

I Love to LAUGH.

Being ready for life merely means that you are ready to take on the responsibilities of being an accountable and law-abiding citizen. Simply put, in addition to having a commitment to understanding the consequences of failing to adhere to rules, policies, and laws; you are now ready for duty and compelled to avoid anything that might potentially threaten your freedom, safety, health, sanity, and ability to engage yourself in the processes of a normal life.

At last, you now have a reasonable level of respect for those who are in a position to enforce rules, policies, and laws. Really, this is called having a newfound level of maturity. You are growing into adulthood and having a smooth transition requires that you be able to respect people with differing opinions, roles, or positions than you.

Sometimes, it will be hard to get along with everyone under the sun. Yes, you will find that it is hard to like everyone you encounter. But the very thought of loving or liking everyone you meet is silly and ridiculous. However, as a mature person it is not much to require that the same level

of respect you extend to someone else is what you should expect in return. So to stay ready for your Best Life, you should always show and give respect to everyone you meet.

Right now, you might be thinking what if someone doesn't respect me first? Glad you asked that... Just know that this predicament may come up. So, practice putting on your game face and commit to not exchanging words, using profanity, making threats of any kind, or physically assaulting someone who says something that is hard to digest or handle. Yep, someday if you haven't already, you will be faced with someone who is not thinking or has not considered your feelings or emotions in any way. *Cool. Life goes on.*

Learn how to ignore things that are not important and people who are insignificant. Yes, words can be hurtful to us, but they can never get up and physically slap or punch us. If you are around someone who becomes enraged or physically combative, just calmly remove yourself from the situation. This isn't running... this is surviving difficult encounters without digesting the <u>extra drama</u> that you don't need.

Honestly, some people need drama in their lives. So you need to consider is this encounter really worth it? Real maturity helps us to resolve that we do not want to be one of those people who can't maintain control over ourselves. Think about it, the adults you truly respect primarily are very good at watching what they say and the kind of

language they use around others. Every now and again you might have that off-the-chain family member who will cuss, fuss, and pick a fight with chocolate on a piece of candy that melted in their pocket overnight. Ignore the foolishness. You have things to do and accomplish.

If you really want to test or challenge yourself, get into the habit of offering good and sound advice to others you think could benefit from hearing that kind of positivity from you. Don't be afraid to shine. Get into the habit of showing others that you are thinking on your feet. ***You woke now...*** *The awakening is real.*

Walking in your newfound level of maturity shows everyone that you know how to react to people who love pulling your emotional strings and triggers. No more do you fly off the handle, physically assault people, use excessive profanity, raise your voice, and refuse to listen to someone who may not agree with something you've said. Now is a great time to adopt the philosophy that two people can agree to disagree. No disrespect, people who are not agreeing on something doesn't ever have to result in violence, discord, disharmony, and hateful antics. Now that you're reading this book, you are turning the corner from actually enjoying tomfoolery. You are much more mature than that now.

If any of these things are truly hard to refrain from doing, it's understood. Just understand the fact that it's okay to

talk to someone who can help you gain better control over yourself, your emotions, and feelings.

BonaFide talk... some people just need help keeping it together. Keeping your "whole" life together requires that you intentionally practice and make habit things that will help you to cope and handle life's ups and downs without you falling apart or worse. It's as simple as that. If people didn't need help from time to time then we wouldn't have the plethora of psychologists, therapists, clinicians, and personal life coaches that we have in the world today. These people are trained to help you find solutions. That's what they do. I will share this, try it before you knock it. Everyone is different. Connection matters, but you should be willing to investigate and consider positive options that will greatly enhance your life. Know that there are tons of professionals who are very good at helping people to get better, stronger, and ready to live their Best Life. Mature men and women already know this.

Once you have made the commitment to stay off the emotional roller coaster that overreacting and impulsivity can sometimes bring, you can now think about where you stand with your education, career training, and job readiness. If you have given up on getting your education together, talk to someone about helping you get whatever you need. Listen, if you seriously want to be considered in today's job market, ask someone you trust how you can get

your high school diploma, GED, a trade certification, associate's degree, or bachelor's degree.

The key is to ASK SOMEONE who either already has the information you need or who can help you find the person who does have the information you're seeking. JUST ASK SOMEONE AND DON'T BE ASHAMED to go after exactly what you need. If you feel *a-certain-kind-of-way* about asking for help, please cut it out. You'll be surprised to find out that people will want to help you with things like this. You can start by confiding in your school counselor, social worker, coach, or administrator. Believe it or not... *someone* on the team really does love kids. That's why they're there every day. Don't assume anything. It's likely that the one person you thought would never help you, may turn out to be the most valuable.

Don't forget that you can always start by going to your local library and asking for help there. Tell the reference or circulation desk what you need and they will definitely assist with finding every resource you need.

Getting on track with your education will no doubt help you to think more about what kind of career or job you'd like to have. Dream a little. Have you met or seen someone on television and envisioned yourself doing the same kind of job? It's normal if you have. So just inquire and ask questions. Be bold about seeking out information that will most definitely change the trajectory of your life. Be a winner and champion on purpose. Nothing will fall out of

the sky and into your lap. Go looking for what you want. Your Best Life Depends on It.

Let's be clear, college isn't for everyone. But getting a job and working is. Am I right about it? Yes, I am. You must work to take care of yourself, your family, and other responsibilities. Figure out what is needed for the job you are interested in. Technical colleges are wonderful, if you haven't already been accepted to a four-year college. Technical colleges provide an incredible amount of worthwhile training and career preparation for many fields of service today.

You may find that certain fields look for a number of their job candidates from specific trade schools and community colleges. If you begin matriculating at a Community College and decide you'd like to apply to a four-year college or university later, you can. This is totally acceptable and encouraged for those who are serious about getting accepted into a specific academic program.

Remember if you decide that you'd rather join the workforce first, it's okay. Go for it. Make sure that you take time to develop your resume, get at least three references, and research the field you think you want to work in. Never go to an interview completely blind. Resolve to know something about the business, its field, and perhaps its market. It just makes sense to know something about the customers who consume their services or products. No longer will you find it acceptable to not raise the bar for

living in our multicultural world and communities. You now understand that you must do things differently if you want to *Live Your Best Life.*

Chapter 18:
Parenting in the New Millennium

If you are a young parent, what I will offer here and now is that you are the most important person in your child's life. No question about it. Who you are and what you are becoming will impact your child and potentially two or three generations of people once you are gone away from here. Think about that. Mothers and fathers both set the trajectory of countless people based on the decisions they make, the risks they take, and their willingness to do something they may have never had the courage to do before.

Your impact as a parent will be remembered for at least 100 years. You can begin starting a family legacy of power and strength based on the decisions you make today. If you know you can use support, a listening ear, and solid resources to activate effective parenting...ASK SOMEONE who is trained to help parents. This is easy and not as hard as you think. If you are a parent and would like to find resources to help you keep-it-together find the resources listed at the back of this book.

Identify people you TRUST whom you can rely on when you need them. If you are a young parent who works or goes to school, find people who might be able to help you with care giving or the supervision of your child when you

are working or in school. Now that you are climbing the ladder to your absolute Best Life, you no longer think about abandoning your child or your responsibilities as a parent. Not even if that happened to you. BONA FIDE talk you must make the firm decision to never forget your painful experiences yet forgive whomever hurt you so that you can be free and unshackled to Live Your Best Life. It's true, awful experiences have a way of webbing hurtful memories that do nothing more than hold us back and at times, make us depressed and cause anxiety. If you experience any of these feelings and emotions, please call someone for help.

As you know, I've been an educator for two decades. My years of experience include my roles as a school social worker, teacher, and principal. Of course, within that time, I have developed a myriad of programs, weekend seminars, and after school activities for parents.

One of my primary interests has always included child wellness and development. In today's world, I am hoping that our parents are paying very close attention to the developmental milestones every child should meet.

According to the Center for Disease Control (CDC) developmental milestones are the continuous growth measures parents can use to track their child's growth and development. Depending on the age range of children, there are varying milestones they should successfully complete and/or experience. Please visit the CDC website at https://www.cdc.gov to read more about childhood

milestones for crawling, rolling over, walking, talking, emotional expressions, and cognitive or learning development. It might be a good idea to think about consulting with your medical doctor, family practitioner, or pediatrician about checking your child's milestone development.

I have included this information for you because the completion of these milestones can help determine if your child is on track with his/her cognitive or learning development. Please know that every child should have specific physical, emotional, communication, and thinking skills. Using the child development milestones are a great place to start if you make the decision to consult a pediatrician about your child's development. This is one of the first steps to managing the development of your child.

As children grow older you or your child's school may notice that he/she has difficulty in meeting certain academic goals or growth milestones. If this should happen, please don't hesitate to consult a professional about these concerns. Your child's school may notice specific things about your child's learning and behavior. At that time, the school will contact you and discuss their findings and ideas for getting your student back on track or on grade level. When you meet with your child's school learn all you can about testing and other services the school offers to help you and your family to understand the current needs of your child. Many states will start this process with

something called SST, which are the abbreviations for Student Support Team.

Schools can offer a wide variety of testing to determine the academic levels of your child. This testing can include many assessments that determine ranges of cognitive development including gifted/talented, autism, and many many more. Remember if you are receiving prenatal care, there are certain test that can be performed while your child is in the womb. Ultimately, I am urging you to be good stewards over your personal health and the health of your children. Ask questions, then ask more questions. Think about it this way, if you find out about something early enough, you can address it. Most importantly, you can understand the best way to improve or avoid any situation.

Chapter 19:
Will the Real Game Changers Please Stand Up!

As I write this, I am thinking about Nipsey Hussle who passed at the age of 33 on March 31, 2019 at the hands of violence in his Los Angeles, California community. Ironically, he was seen as a modern-day warrior, someone who impacted his community by providing resources, support, and answers.

Now, that's a Game Changer,

NO CAP!

He was someone who lived in the very community he wanted to help lift, pull, and push to higher heights. He had a vision that included seeing lower income people find ways and means to legitimately come up, whether through better schools, more jobs, affordable housing, and safer communities... he was an advocate.

Nipsey Hussle was a true statesman who had an incredible ability to help every man and woman in his community to hear so that they could invariably be heard. He believed in creating win-win situations for everyone, that's what an authentic game changer does. This warrior for all intents

and purposes believed that things could be better in his community. He saw the challenges and decided he would meet those challenges with resolutions that made sense.

Historically, that's how we saw our warriors. They were providers, protectors, and in some regard... priest. They were set apart. Leaders, chiefs, generals, or captains. They took charge of things. They felt it was incumbent upon them to protect their land, community, and neighborhood. That's really what they were.

Now, here we are at the beginning of a brand-new decade. As we take a deeper look at our Millennial generation or the post millennial generation it appears they've somehow lost their cultural focus, compass, intentions, and purpose. Why do I say that?

Honestly, when you consider the ever-increasing episodes of violence and crime in our communities, one might wonder where are the warriors amongst us? *BonaFide Talk* we have countless reports which suggest that many of our warriors have taken a nap on the concept of actually avoiding things, people, and activities that do not change the conditions or trajectory of the people who are suffering from their personal living and mental health conditions.

The millennials have taken a new stance on life. This is that generation you cannot just throw old-school concepts, philosophies, and ideas upon. It is a fact that you will be wasting your time, if you do that. Perfect example are the

skill sets that older generations were convinced that they needed to be successful in life. Today, many of the millennials are challenged with not having patience, team spirit, a good work ethic, problem solving, or customer service skills. Seriously, my millennials admit that it is common for young people to stay ready to fight, argue, or worse. Going even further, according to some millennials... due to their lack of patience, propensity to argue with coworkers and maybe customers, they opt to merely engage in illegal or criminal activities to make their money. Of course, that's nothing new... NO CAP! People do resort to things that are risky, dangerous, and sometimes illegal to survive.

Being someone from a BONA FIDE HOOD, I am here to announce that **YOU CAN DO BETTER**. And of course, just because you're from a "hood" the "hood" doesn't have to be in you.

For clarity, the neighborhood I was raised in has been characterized as one of the largest urban centers in the country. This simply boils down to being a big major city which shares water and boundary lines with New York City. Trust me when I tell you that you don't have enough time to read all the names of the warriors and others who survived "the hood" without resorting to things which threatened their very existence. I call that throwing the dice. The kiss and blow effect. When we take the route of not caring and not considering positive options, ways, and

choices to resolve our challenges... it usually doesn't offer a helpful outcome for anyone.

Ultimately, Ready or Not, my millennials can take the chess game of their life and achieve check mate in record time when they master a few qualities that are sure to inform their opinions about **finding their purpose** in life, knowing their identity, and understanding the **importance of planning** for their Best Life.

The millennial game changers have proven that they have an impressive capacity to impact change or at least influence others in ridiculous numbers. The world of technology has been your friend. The invention of social media has helped you to start relationships, end relationships, plan events, play digital games with others who are far away, start businesses, make money, collaborate ideas with others, complete educational pursuits, and keep the lines of communication open across many area codes. This has been your era. You have single handedly advanced what others started while you were still running around in pampers and onesies.

When you think about life... your life, I am urging you to think about how you might help to create positive changes for yourself and others. It is important for you to understand that your life is not just for you... you should be able to do something to either lighten or brighten someone else's life or life experiences. That's what a true game changer does. He or she uses his/her skills and tools to talk

and communicate with others, make worthwhile plans for his life, be *intentional* about staying encouraged, and have the courage to keep doing something until you see the results you were hoping for.

Winning at this Life Game requires that you **think**, consider consequences to every decision you make. Long lasting or sometimes life changing consequences to what you're doing. Remember, life as in the game of chess requires much contemplation. You are constantly strategizing, thinking, and considering how your decisions might impact more than just you.

As the millennials cope more with the differences they possess, including their short comings and opinions, they are constantly trying to do whatever it takes to win-the-game. When life gets over whelming, just remember to get in a quiet place, take out a piece of paper and something to write with, then **visualize** and proceed to map out your **life plan**.

Plan it out- before you walk it out.

Chapter 20:
HELP IS JUST A PHONE CALL AWAY

Over time, students are given a lot of information. Starting in elementary school through senior year of high school students are provided with a wealth of information. At times, health and fitness teachers will discuss a wide variety of topics relevant and appropriate for elementary, middle or high school students. Athletic coaches may also discuss topics related to the personal growth, health, and wellness of their athletes and students.

Helping teenagers and young adults maintain balance in their lives is of paramount interest. As you mature, grow older, and continue to have many questions about life and having a normal experience both in and outside of school, you are bound to have one or more questions. I have found that many of my students often refrain from asking personal questions due to their mixed feelings of insecurity, embarrassment, or distrust. In some instances, students had feelings about things, but had no idea how to appropriately broach the topic with a school teacher, administrator, or coach.

The thought of finding answers to certain private or very personal questions can be daunting to say the least. As teenagers and young adults work hard to keep their life vision on the radar, while maintaining positive relationships with others can still bring reasonable levels of stress or anxiety to a young person's life. Of course, having a great

mentor can certainly help make your life's journey less difficult, however there may be an occasion when you need the attention, help, and support of a professional who doesn't know you.

Unfortunately, in life there are people who are confronted with hardship or despair due to nothing they did. Sadly enough, people become innocent bystanders to the despair, misery, or pain of someone else. It happens more often than we care to count. Truthfully, some teens and other young people can feel trapped or forced to endure harmful situations when they are either *fearful or too embarrassed to talk about it with someone they know.*

The opportunity to discuss problems in a confidential manner becomes even more difficult for the young person who has not identified a trusted mentor, coach, teacher, counselor, or another adult to simply *talk* with. Having the space and freedom to be yourself and transparent is liberating. Having a platform to be honest and open with a trusted adult will certainly afford you a strong chance to consider other sound opinions or perceptions of a wide variety of scenarios and situations.

If you haven't found anyone in your life that you can trust and **talk** with... then this chapter will be helpful to you if you're dealing with a serious situation and would like to discuss it openly with certified or licensed professionals who are trained and qualified to share information, services, and resources with you.

It is a fact that many teenagers have little to no ideas about who or where to call should they find themselves in an emergency situation that requires immediate attention. This chapter is dedicated to the young people who are willing to ask questions, find answers, and start conversations by contacting the professionals who provide the kind of services you need.

In this chapter, you will find a pocket- sized directory for organizations and agencies that provide a wide array of help and answers to questions you might have. Always try talking with an adult you know and trust first. Remember there are safe hangouts where you can go if you need help or a place to stay. If you want assistance and would like an adult to talk with, you might consider finding someone at your local recreation/ community center, church, or after school program. Don't forget you can also find a good confidant in some of your other trusted family members who may not live near you. If you're not feeling comfortable enough to talk directly with your parent or guardian, please find another trusted adult to talk with.

Most importantly, remember to think before you act. Don't ever make a serious decision about anything before talking with someone you trust. Remember... hearing another perspective can be very helpful. Myself, I love talking with older people, like older than my mom. They are so precious and very wise. *Trust and Believe*, they know stuff! So, you can always talk to a grandparent, older family member, or senior citizen in your neighborhood.

If you think you still don't have anyone to talk to, then there are hotlines and organizations listed that are available to help with many concerns affecting youth today. Please check the hours of operation when you call each agency.

You can take notes at the back of this book.

QUESTIONS ABOUT SEX

When you're thinking about <u>not having sex</u> and you want to talk with someone about abstaining from sex, there are agencies that can provide you support with abstaining.

Abstinence/ HHS.gov
U.S. Department of Health & Human Services
1-877-696-6775
24 hours a day/ 7 days a week

Sexual Abstinence: Making the Right Choice
Website: www.hrmvideo.com
1-800-431-2050
7am- 9pm

National Campaign to Prevent Teen and Unplanned Pregnancy
1-800-230-PLAN
Provides information to teens about abstinence, sex, love, and healthy relationships.
https://www.plannedparenthood.org/

Gravity
(1-800-230-7526) 1-800-230-PLAN
A phone hotline and online hotline offers anonymous answers to questions about abstinence, sexual behaviors, relationships and communicating with your parents.
www.gravityteen.org

Sex Sense/ Options for Sexual Health
Ask questions about sex and sexuality, etc. Talk with
experts at 1-800-739-7367 Visit Website:
www.optionsforsexualhealth.org

Centers for Disease Control (CDC) info
800-232-4636 (800-CDC-INFO)
24 hours a day/ 7 days a week
Visit Website:www.cdc.gov

GLBT National Youth Talkline
800-246-7743 (PRIDE)
Visit Website: www.glnh.org/talkline

QUESTIONS ABOUT
SEXUALLY TRANSMITTED DISEASES

STD Hotline
800-227-8922
www.ashastd.org
Find answers to frequently asked questions about sexually
transmitted infections and hook up with a support group in
your area.

Teens and AIDS Hotline
1-800-440-TEEN
A hotline specifically for teens living with HIV/AIDS or
for teens with questions about HIV/AIDS.

National AIDS Hotline
800-342-2437
800-344-7432 (en espanol)
www.ashastd.org/nah/tty.html
Ask your questions about HIV/AIDS and read up on
important things to know if you're a teen living with HIV.

National Herpes Hotline
919-361-8488
www.herpesonline.org
Provides support for emotional issues surrounding herpes.

AIDSinfo
1-800-448-0440 (Monday-Friday 12 noon- 5pm EST
HopeLine
Call or TEXT 919-231-4525 or 1-877-235-4525

Teen Growth
www.teengrowth.com/
This is a website of choice for thousands of teens looking
for health information.
TeensHealth.com
www.teenshealth.com
A helpful website designed by professional for developing
pre-teens, adolescents, teenagers and young adults.

The Society for Adolescent Medicine
www.adolescenthealth.org
Provides health information and resources to pre-
adolescents and adolescents.

QUESTIONS ABOUT HEALTH AND HYGIENE

American Medical Association
http://www.ama-assn.org
Provides medical information on adolescence.
American Pediatric Association
www.aap.org
Provides information and resources on adolescent health.
Center for Disease Control –Division of Adolescent and
School Health
1-800-227-8922
www.cdc.gov

DASH provides information on reducing and preventing
health risk behaviors among children, adolescents and
young adults.

4 Girls Health
http://www.4girls.gov
Provides health information and resources for girls-only.

QUESTIONS ABOUT ABUSE, BULLYING, SCHOOL VIOLENCE AND DISCRIMINATION

Discrimination and Anti-Hate Line
1-800-649-0404

National Coalition Against Domestic Violence Hotline (24 hours)
1-800-799-SAFE (1-800-799-7233)
www.ncadv.org

NATIONAL CHILD ABUSE HOTLINE
1-800-422-4453
www.childhelp.org
A trained counselor will tell you how to get help if you have been sexually and physically abused. The call is free and answered 24 hours a day.

NATIONAL CAMPAIGN AGAINST YOUTH VIOLENCE
1-800-99-YOUTH
www.violencepreventionweek.org
This group encourages teens to use outlets other than violence to express themselves. The site offers tips for preventing violence and information to start anti-violence projects in your community.

NATIONAL CLEARINGHOUSE ON CHILD ABUSE AND NEGLECT INFORMATION
1-800-394-3366
http://nccanch.acf.hhs.gov

NATIONAL RESOURCE CENTER ON DOMESTIC
VIOLENCE
1-888-Rx-Abuse
http://endabuse.org

NATIONAL SEXUAL VIOLENCE RESOURCE
CENTER (NSVRC)
1-877-739-3895
www.nsvrc.org
www.teenpcar.com
This organization provides information, support, and help
for teen victims of sexual violence.

RAPE, ABUSE, AND INCEST NATIONAL NETWORK
(RAINN)
1-800-656-HOPE www.rainn.or
If you have been sexually assaulted, have a friend who has
been sexually assaulted, or want to know how to reduce
your risk of sexual assault, RAINN is where you want to
turn.

QUESTIONS ABOUT ADOPTION

National Adoption Center
1-800-862-3678
http://www.adopt.org/

QUESTIONS ABOUT
ALCOHOL, DRUGS, and TOBACCO
ADDICTIONS AND TREATMENT

Addictions
1-888-762-3750
Find assistance with intervention, referral and treatment services.
www.nationalhotline.org

Alcohol and Drug Abuse Help Line
1-800-821-4357
A national hotline that answers 24 hours a day,7 days a week. Someone will tell you about alcohol and drug abuse organizations in your area. The call is free and very confidential.
Alcohol and Drug Abuse Help Line

American Council on Alcoholism
1-800-527-534 www.aca-usa.org
A national hotline that answers calls from 8am-4pm, Monday-Friday. Leave a message after 4pm.

Alcohol
1-800-NCA-CALL (1-800-622-2255)
National Council on Alcoholism (24 hours)
Helpline for finding treatment.

Al-Anon
1-800-356-9996
www.al-anon.org

Support group meetings. Help for people who need to deal with family members and friends who are recovering from alcoholism.

AlaTeen
1-888-425-2666
www.al-anon.org
Recovery program for young people struggling with alcoholism.
Cocaine and Crack Hotline
1-800-COCAINE

Provides assistance 24 hours a day to individuals struggling with cocaine and crack addictions.
Cocaine Anonymous
1-800-347-8998
Provides counseling and referral services for individuals struggling with cocaine addictions.

Freevibe
www.freevibe.com
This site is located with stats on teen drug and alcohol abuse. Send a "Buzz" to a friend, post messages on the boards, read true stories about teens with drug problems, and share your own stories.

Marijuana Anonymous
1-800-766-6779
Provides counseling and referral services for individuals struggling with marijuana addictions.

National Clearinghouse for Alcohol and Drug Information. 1-800-729-6686 Call here for resources on alcohol and drug abuse treatment.

Tobacco Use
The American Cancer Society
www.cancer.org
This website provides teens with information on youth tobacco prevention.

QUESTIONS ABOUT
YOUR MENTAL HEALTH
IF YOU REALLY NEED TO TALK TO SOMEONE

CRISIS CALL CENTER
for mental health, homelessness, loneliness, sexual health, and more.
(601-713-4357) 601-713-HELP
A helpline for adolescents in crisis.

Youth Suicide Prevention Services
(Teen Link)

1-888-431-8336. 6p-10p

1-800-852-8336. 9p-1a EST

1-800-843-5200 Youth Crisis Line 24/7

Provides information and resources for youth suicide prevention.

Online Individual Counseling
Visit Website at **www.betterhelp.com**
An online counseling platform with licensed therapists.
Contact them and inquire about how you can receive support.

National Mental Health Association
1-800-969-6642 9am-5pm EST
www.nmha.org/ www.mentalhealthamerica.net

Mental health support for anxiety disorders, depression, attention deficit, suicidal thoughts, and substance abuse. Has over 300 affiliates nationwide. They are happy to talk with anyone who feels they need a listening ear.

ALL CALLS ARE CONFIDENTIAL

National Suicide Hotline
Crisis Calls for Grief and Loss
(1-800-273-8255). 1-800-273-TALK
www.suicidepreventionlifeline.org

24 hours per day/ 7 days per week
Provides free and confidential suicide prevention and supportive services.
Crisis Text Line
Text the word HELLO to 741741
You can text chat with a Crisis Counselor.

QUESTIONS ABOUT GRIEF SUPPORT AND EDUCATION

Teen Support Place
www.teensupportplace.org
www.griefsupportservices.org

An online grief support group for adolescents and teens.

Shining Light
www.myshininglight.com
954-827-0295

Provides grief support to teens and their families.

QUESTIONS ABOUT SELF-ESTEEM

TeensHealth.com
Visit this helpful website to learn more about improving
your self-esteem and feeling good about yourself.

QUESTIONS ABOUT
HOMELESSNESS

Covenant House Crisis Hotline
1-800-999-9999
www.covenanthouse.org
A national crisis hotline for youth. The call is free. They
answer 24 hours a day, 7 days a week and can provide
referrals and offer crisis counseling on many topics.

Girls and Boys Town National Hotline
1-800-448-3000
www.girlsandboystown.org
A crisis hotline for teens. The free and confidential call is
answered 24 hours a day, 7 days a week. They offer
problem solving on any issue and encourage teens to talk to
their parents or caretakers about issues that may require
professional assistance.

National Runaway Switchboard
1-800-621-4000
National crisis hotline for runaways and homeless youth.

QUESTIONS ABOUT
DATING AND RELATIONSHIPS

Love Is Respect
1-866-331-9474
www.loveisrespect.org
Provides information and resources on healthy teen
relationships.

TeensHealth.com
Visit this Website: www.teenshealth.com
For helpful information about teenagers, including body,
mind, sexual health, fitness, and diseases.

QUESTIONS ABOUT DISABILITIES AND DISCRIMINATION

Discrimination and Anti-Hate Line
1-800-649-0404
Provides assistance with discrimination and hate problems.

Disabilities and Discrimination
Hotline
1- 800-426-HAND
Provides information about discrimination to individuals
with special health care needs.

Minority Health Resource Center
800-444-6472
www.omhrc.gov
An informative public health site which focuses on issues
affecting American Indians and Alaska Natives, Asian,
Americans, Native Hawaiians and other Pacific Islanders,
Black/African Americans, and Hispanics/Latinos.

QUESTIONS ABOUT GETTING EDUCATION

EDUCATION AND SCHOOL
National Dropout Prevention Center
1-800-656-2599
www.dropoutprevention.org
Provides information on the importance of staying in school.

QUESTIONS ABOUT
SCHOOL VIOLENCE AND BULLYING

Speak Up
1-866- 773-2587
24 hours a day/ 7 days a week

Thursday's Child National Youth Advocacy Hotline
800-872-5437
24 hours a day/ 7 days a week

QUESTIONS ABOUT NUTRITION, OBESITY, BODY IMAGE AND PHYSICAL FITNESS

National Eating Disorders Association
1-800-931-2237
www.nationaleatingdisorders.org
Receive teen-friendly information about eating disorders. The calls are free and answered from 10am - 7pm, Monday to Friday.

National Association of Anorexia Nervosa and Associated Disorders
1-847-831-3438
www.anad.org

Pick up free hotline counseling and learn about support groups for sufferers and families of people with eating disorders. You'll also find referrals to health care professionals who treat eating disorders across the U.S. and in fifteen other countries.

QUESTIONS ABOUT
FINDING RESOURCES FOR TEEN PARENTS

TeenLine
(310)855-4673
(800)852-8336
TEXT the word TEEN to 839863

Crisis Text Line
TEXT the word HELLO to 741741
24 hours a day/ 7 days a week

Boys Town National Hotline
1-800-448-3000
http://www.boystown.org/hotline

Planned Parenthood Federation of America
800-230-PLAN
www.plannedparenthood.org
Get information about teen reproductive health, teen
pregnancy and parenting issues. You can also get
connected with a clinic near you.

National Center on Early Childhood Health and wellness
888-227-5125
You can send questions and request for information to
health@ecetta
Crisis Call Center
1-800-273-8255. or
TEXT the word ANSWER to 839863
24 hours a day/ 7 days a week

American Pregnancy Helpline
1-866-6466
24 hours a day/ 7 days a week
http://www.thehelpline.org

lanned Parenthood Federation of America
800-230-PLAN
www.plannedparenthood.org
Find information about teen reproductive health, teen
pregnancy and parenting issues. You can also get
connected with a clinic near you.

Centers for Disease Control
800-227-8922
www.cdc.gov
The official governmental health site and clearinghouse for
adolescent health statistics. Also includes health
information for the consumer. Extensive information about
HIV/AIDS, other STDs, and other adolescent health
matters.

Baby Safe Haven
Confidential toll free hotline at (888) 510-2229.
You can call *ANONYMOUSLY* to get information about
giving up an unwanted child without arrest or legal
prosecution. Call to get your questions answered.

ALL CALLS ARE CONFIDENTIAL.

SERIOUS IMMEDIATE EMERGENCIES

Remember, if you are currently in an emergency or someone you know is in danger, please contact your local law enforcement agency by dialing "911" for EMERGENCIES ONLY or dial "0" for an (Operator) in an emergency and give your location, including your county, city, and the address where help is needed.

911 or 0 for Emergencies Only (Ambulance/Fire/Police)

77 on Cell Phones for Emergencies Only (Ambulance/Fire/Police)

Suicide Hotline: 1-800-784-2433

Crisis Call Center: 1-800-273-8255 or text the word ANSWER to 83986

<u>Disclaimer</u>

The resources and contact information provided in this book have been provided for your convenience. When using this information, if needed, you can check the accuracy of the contact information by utilizing your favorite search engine *(ie. Google or Bing)*.
In the event that an agency has changed its location, phone contact, email or website address please remember to <u>check online</u> for the most current contact information.

Thank You

Hosea Strong, Artist
Atlanta, Georgia
2020

References

Across Ages LoSciuto, L., Rajala, A., Townsend, T. N., & Taylor, A. S. (1996). An outcome evaluation of Across Ages: An intergenerational mentoring approach to drug prevention. Journal of Adolescent Research, 11(1), 116-129. Aseltine, R., Dupre, M., & Lamlein, P. (2000). Mentoring as a drug prevention strategy:An evaluation of Across Ages. Adolescent and Family Health, 1, 11-20. Big Brothers/Big SistersTierney, J. P., Grossman, J. B., & Resch, N. L. (1995). Making a difference: An impact study of Big Brothers/Big Sisters. Philadelphia: Public/Private Ventures. Morrow, K. V. & Styles, M. B. (1995). Building Relationships with youth in program settings: A study of Big Brothers/Big Sisters. Philadelphia: Public/Private Ventures. Rhodes, J., Grossman, J., & Resch, N. (2000). Agents of change: Pathways through which mentoring relationships influence adolescents' academic adjustment. Child Development,71, 1662-1671. Furano, K., Roaf, P. A., Styles, M. B., & Branch, A. Y. (1993). Big Brothers/Big Sisters: A study of program practices. Philadelphia: Public/Private Ventures. Grossman, J. B. & Rhodes, J. E. (1999). The test of time: Predictors and effects of duration in youth mentoring relationships. Unpublished manuscript. The Buddy System Fo, W. S. O., & O'Donnell, C. (1975). The Buddy System: Effect of community intervention on delinquent offenses. Behavior Therapy, 6, 522-524. O'Donnell, C.R., Lydgate, T., & Fo, W.S.O. (1979). The Buddy System: Review and follow-up. Child Behavior Therapy, 1(2), 161-169.

My Final Note...

I hope this little book of life's pearls will help millennials, preteens and others to realize their Best Life. Then... hopefully you will help someone else live their Best Life too.

Thank You for Reading!
Dr. Isaac

#SECURE THE QUEEN
&
#ALWAYS TREASURE THE KING

Acknowledgements

First, I give THANKS and HONOR to **GOD ALMIGHTY** for giving me this gift and passion for writing. My prayer is that this work be used to help as many youth as possible. I do appreciate the opportunity to provide this information and resources that can be used to empower millennials and other generations to be winners in life. A very special thanks go to my students who are the millennials I've taught and have in some way *inspired* me to write this book.

Big appreciation goes to **Dr. E. Dewey Smith, Senior Pastor/ Teacher of The House of Hope Atlanta.** Much Luv goes to **my pastor and the entire church family** who works so tirelessly to respond to the needs of families, children in crisis, and adults who need support. I'm proud of everything you do for our community. I'm praying that the Perfect 2020 Vision and Will of GOD continues to be realized in my heart and service for **ALL** youth. …Always **Believing** that the information shared in this book is a Blessing to everyone who reads it.

My incredibly awesome family which I deem to be one of the strongest of Lone Cypress trees imagined. **Our family** has the most beautiful branches which stretch deep and wide from the robust trunk of the **ENTIRE Owens family** in Yazoo and Hinds County Mississippi and connects

straight onto the branches of the **Isaac**, **Fuqua**, **Polk**, **Dillon**, **Washington**, and **Wilks** tribes. Along with the Owens family, I would also like to thank my entire **Goodman family** for their love and support. All of you who know me, have shown me endless love and encouragement over the years. You have all inspired me to never give up and lean on God in everything that I do. When I think of all of the people in my life whom I see as true family, I can't forget the **Gilmore**, **Bentley**, **Hartfield**, **Maple**, **West**, and **Youngblood** families. You each have a special lock on my heart.

NO CAP!

I have the most loving family ever.

My BFF, **Anita Van Hook** who is truly my sister all the way from **Rutgers University,** *Livingston College known as "the Rock"* to this very day. ...I'm talking 36 years. Decades and decades of laughs, talks, debates, and unforgettable memories. She's my **FAM** too! Gotta give big love to my Georgia Sis, **Dr. Vicki Austell-Henderson**. She's my second think tank on-deck from **CAU**. Thanks ladies for helping me to chop up all the BIG Ideas I often seem to have. Thanks for listening, supporting, and being my true sisters. You keep me encouraged to own the race, no matter how tough it gets at times.

A very special shout out goes to **Ms. Colleen Bell** who works so tirelessly with our students. Keep up the great

work that you do with our students and other creative projects you have! **Jordan Reid**, your graphic arts skills are stellar!! Thank you for your contributions to this work. I'm praying that much success follows you throughout your entire life. You are a great talent and you make us all very proud.

I would be remiss if I didn't thank past and present colleagues and dynamic supervisors. It's just something about those educators…

You all are the BEST!!

A very special thanks goes to the school administrators whom I have appreciated your kindness, encouragement, mentorship, and faith to do a-good-work for our students. Whether I work with you now or in the past, I will never forget you. **Bulldog Nation** *(Tri Cities High School of East Point, Georgia)* and the **Mighty Knights** *(Frank McClarin High School of College Park, Georgia)* are the real awesome sauce of urban schools today! A loud shout out goes to the Astro's of **Frederick Douglass High School** in APS too! I've had incredible students at each school.
Love U!

Mr. Brown… *YOU DID THAT!!* The one school principal who truly made it possible for me to become a school administrator. I am forever grateful. You are a wonderful role model and mentor. There was a lot to

acknowledge you for during your tenure at Douglass High School, but you are now a Blue Ribbon School Principal in Virginia. You make us all so proud!

Ms. Bailey, my girl! You are a hard-working dynamo. Incredible educator and school leader. Any school would be lucky to have you whether you're in Georgia or Texas, I know you're making a great difference.

Along with Mr. Brown, I must give a special shout out to my phenomenal **Sands, Lesley Jones Sessler**. I will never ever forget the confidence, love, and support you have shown me throughout my career as an educator. You are dynamic in your own right. Thank you for being the incredible woman, educator, and school leader that you are. Sands You Are Truly A Force To Be Reckoned With!! There is no doubt that all of my Sands are pretty incredible. That's why they call us

The Untouchables of Delta Sigma Theta Sorority, Inc.
Big Love to Lil Sis Kioka Jones!!

Gina Gee thanks for making me laugh! You are truly my lil' sistah who keeps a smile in her heart and always something witty to say. Always! *Get That Book Ready Guuurl!!!*

Bryan Cannon, school administrator extraordinaire, thanks for being a true friend and a progressive school leader. Over the years, you've done so much to put a distinguished

mark of excellence on helping students excel to higher and higher heights. You are a treasured educator. Keep doing the fantastic job that you do for schools each and every day.

Pastor, Dr. Ieisha Marion, I'm very proud of you! You've allowed GOD to come in your heart and do great works for his kingdom. Your faith, wisdom, energy, creativity, and sense of innovation is endless. Keep on using your gifts and talents to Bless God's People. Your ministry is needed, and I pray that GOD will continue to use, keep, and Bless you beyond measure. I've known you since second grade at Saint Patrick's Elementary School in Jersey City. We were classmates in elementary, high school, and college. I thank GOD that you are actually one of my oldest friends who really has known me my entire life. Where has the time gone? Many Blessings to YOU Sis and Keep on Fighting the Good Fight!!

My favorite teacher, **Mrs. Davis**. I really hope that this book makes you proud. Thank you for being more than a teacher. You inspired and empowered me to dream and actually think that I could do whatever I set my mind to. Thank you for being so much more than a teacher!

Last but not least, my **#1 mentor, Ms. Terrie M. Williams**, the *PR Guru of all time*. **She is the *GOAT*!** Not only is my now retired mentor nationally known as a world class entertainment publicist, but she is also an award-winning author. Hands down, you have supported me from the very beginning of my professional career starting at

Essence Magazine in 1988. You have been there to encourage, inspire, drive, and keep me in check for more than thirty years. It is amazing that I have remained friends with you and most of those whom worked with me at the **Terrie Williams Agency** (Chris Cathcart, Taren Mitchell Fleming, Evelyn Evans-Oliver, DeAnna Lenz, CJ Harris, Nicole Scott (Rainbow), Lucretia Scott, Ghana Wilson, Jean Owensby (*RIP*), Ryan Stewart, and Carl McCaskill.) You had the hardest working, dynamic, and most creative PR team in all of New York City. I miss you all so much.

Because of you Terrie, I have had the most exciting and **unmatched** professional experiences of anyone I know. You introduced me to the world of entertainment with exposure to countless projects, events, and campaigns that I will forever treasure in my life. Thank you for being the awesome sauce *Queen Mentor* that you are.

I love you!

About the Author

Dr. Bridget Isaac is a native of New Jersey. She is an alum of Rutgers University where she earned a bachelor's degree in Journalism. After moving to Georgia, this life coach and educator completed both her masters and doctoral degree studies at Clark Atlanta University. Earning degrees and substantial training in the areas of School Social Work and Educational Leadership prepared her for the various roles she has successfully fulfilled as a school social worker, mental health therapist, teacher, and school principal. She is truly a renaissance woman who is never afraid to pursue exactly what she has passion and zeal for.

As her professional endeavors and interest grew, she has been led on some of the most life changing and rewarding experiences imagined. No matter how challenging the path may have been, her professional adventures always

invariably led her back to serving youth and their families. Across more than two decades, she has ignited her innovative ideas, energy, and commitment to the fields of publishing, broadcast media, the recording industry, public relations, social work, education, and now life coaching. Never a dull moment for this Renaissance woman who loves working with people and strives to be an agent of change in everything that she does. Dr. Isaac currently lives in Atlanta, Georgia where she enjoys her work as an educator, life coach, speaker, and author.

Your Notes Go Here

_____

_____

_____

_____

_____

_____

_____

_____

_____

_____

_____

_____

_____

_____

_____

_____

_____

_____

_____

_____

_____

_____

_____

_____

_____

_____

_____

_____

Your Notes Go Here

Your Notes Go Here

Your Notes Go Here

ISBN: 978-0-578-63297-1
Publisher: Talk Bonafide Media LLC
Lanuage: English
Page Count: 164
Size: 5X8
Genre: Young Adult Non Fiction
Format: Paperback

For information about this book
Please contact the publisher at
Talk Bonafide Media LLC
3355 Lenox Road
Suite 750
Atlanta, Georgia 30326

Made in the USA
Columbia, SC
07 November 2021